P • C

WORLD ATLAS

D0456532

CZECH REPUBLIC

LAOS

PAKISTAN

JAMAICA

SAO TOME AND PRINCIPE

SOLOMON ISLAND

CANADA

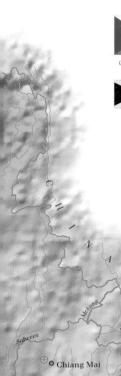

C H I N A

Black R.

Red R.

L. Thac Ba

Viet Tri

Thai Nguyen

HANOI

Hong Gai

Hai Phong

Nam Ou

Mekong

Mekong

Louang Phrabang

Nam Dinh

Thanh Hoa

V I E T N A M

Gulf of Tongking

L A O S

Saloeen

Chiang Mai

Nam Theun

Vinh

VIENTIANE

Udon Thani

Muang Phitsanulok

P · O · C · K · E · T · S

WORLD ATLAS

Written by
ESTHER LABI

DORLING KINDERSLEY
London • New York • Stuttgart

A DORLING KINDERSLEY BOOK

Editor	Esther Labi
Designer	Carlton Hibbert
Senior editor	Hazel Egerton
Senior art editor	Jacquie Gulliver
Editorial consultant	Joan Dear
Picture research	Lorna Ainger
Production	Ruth Cobb
US Editor	Jill Hamilton

First American Edition, 1995
2 4 6 8 10 9 7 5 3 1
Published in the United States by
Dorling Kindersley Publishing, Inc.,
95 Madison Avenue,
New York, New York 10016

Library of Congress Cataloging-in-Publication Data

Labi, Esther.
World atlas / written by Esther Labi. – – 1st Amer. ed.
p. cm. – – (Pockets)
Includes index.
Summary: A comprehensive atlas to the countries of the world.
ISBN 0-7894-0215-7
1. Children's atlases. [1. Atlases.] I. Title. II. Series.
G1021.D4 1995 <G&M>

912 – – dc20   95 – 148
                                                      CIP
                                                      MAP AC

Color reproduction by Colourscan, Singapore
Printed and bound in Italy by L.E.G.O.

CONTENTS

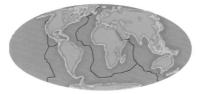

HOW TO USE THIS BOOK

THESE PAGES SHOW YOU how to use *Pockets: World Atlas*. The maps are organized by continent: North America, Central and South America, Europe, Africa, North and West Asia, South and East Asia, and Australasia. There is also an introductory section at the front and a comprehensive index at the back.

KEY TO ICONS
All the icons used in the Atlas are listed below.

🎵 THE ARTS

☁ CLIMATE

📶 COMMUNICATIONS

☣ ENVIRONMENT

🦋 FLORA AND FAUNA

🏛 HISTORY

🏭 INDUSTRY

⛰ NATURAL FEATURES

👪 PEOPLE

Heading

Introduction

Locator map

Grid reference

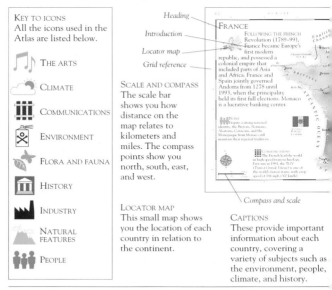

FRANCE
FOLLOWING THE FRENCH
Revolution (1789–99),
France became Europe's
first modern
republic, and possessed a
colonial empire that
included parts of Asia
and Africa. France and
Spain jointly governed
Andorra from 1278 until
1993, when the principality
held its first full elections. Monaco
is a lucrative banking center.

Compass and scale

SCALE AND COMPASS
The scale bar shows you how distance on the map relates to kilometers and miles. The compass points show you north, south, east, and west.

LOCATOR MAP
This small map shows you the location of each country in relation to the continent.

CAPTIONS
These provide important information about each country, covering a variety of subjects such as the environment, people, climate, and history.

NTRODUCTION
This provides you with
n overview of the
rea or region and
ives interesting facts
about the country's
limate, landscape,
nd political situation.

RUNNING HEADS
These remind you which
section you are in. At the
top of the left-hand page
is the name of the
continent. The right-
hand page gives the
country. These pages on
France are in the section
on Europe.

Running head

— *Caption icon*

— *Caption*

CLIMATE
France is
mostly temperate, but
summers in the
south are dry, sunny,
and hot. In the
Pyrenees and
Alps, cooler
mountain
climate prevails.

INDUSTRY
Tourism,
engineering,
wine, aerospace.
France is a world
leader in cosmetics,
wine, and perhaps
the-Jans farmers
produce over 300
types of cheese.

FLAGS
The flag of each
nation is positioned
next to the country.
Also included are
population figures
(**P**) and information
about the official
languages spoken in
that area (**L**).

Flag

GRID REFERENCE
The letters and numbers
round this grid help you
ocate places listed in the
ndex. See page 136 for
n explanation on how to
se this grid.

GAZETTEER INDEX
A gazetteer index at the
back of the book lists all the
major towns, cities, rivers,
mountain ranges, and lakes
that appear in the book.

INTERNATIONAL
BORDER

DISPUTED
BORDER

STATE BORDER

CAPITAL CITY — SHING'T
D.C.

STATE OR
ADMINISTRATIVE — LANTA
CAPITAL

MAJOR TOWN — arlesto

AIRPORT

SEAPORT

RIVER

CANAL

WADI

LAKE

SEASONAL LAKE

GUIDE TO MAP PAGES

EUROPE
54-55

NORTH AND
WEST ASIA
102-103

SOUTH AND
EAST ASIA
114-115

AFRICA
86-87

*INDIAN
OCEAN*

*ATLANTIC
OCEAN*

AUSTRALASIA
130-131

*SOUTHERN
OCEAN*

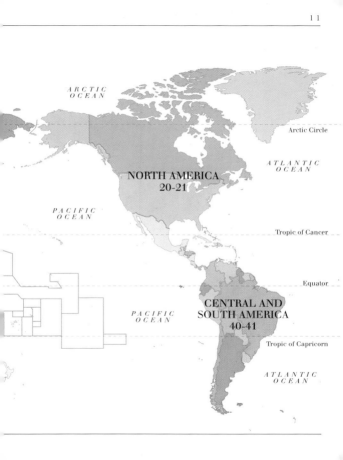

ARCTIC
OCEAN

Arctic Circle

ATLANTIC
OCEAN

NORTH AMERICA
20-21

PACIFIC
OCEAN

Tropic of Cancer

Equator

PACIFIC
OCEAN

CENTRAL AND
SOUTH AMERICA
40-41

Tropic of Capricorn

ATLANTIC
OCEAN

THE PLANET EARTH

EARTH, ONE OF nine planets that travel around the Sun, is part of the solar system within a galaxy called the Milky Way. The only planet within our solar system that supports life, Earth has sufficient light, heat, and water to support a wide range of plants and animals. The atmosphere protects the planet by filtering the Sun's rays.

Inner core

Outer core

Mantle

Crust

People once thought that the Earth was completely solid

Earth's surface

EARTH'S STRUCTURE
The Earth has four major layers: the crust, mantle, and outer and inner core. The crust, made up of soil and rock, and the molten outer layer of the mantle compose the lithosphere. The inner layer of the mantle is solid, like the inner core, while the outer core is thick fluid.

THE MOON

A ball of barren rock, the Moon orbits the Earth every 27.3 days. The Moon's gravity exerts a powerful pull on Earth. The Moon and Sun together create tides in the Earth's oceans. The highest tides occur twice a month when the Moon, Sun, and Earth are aligned.

Craters are caused by meteor collisions

EARTH'S ROTATION

Every 23 hours, 56 minutes, and 4 seconds the Earth rotates once on its axis. This makes any point on Earth face alternately toward and away from the Sun, producing day and night. Seasons are caused by each hemisphere leaning toward or away from the Sun on the Earth's 365.242-day orbit.

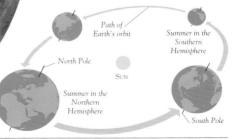

Path of Earth's orbit

Summer in the Southern Hemisphere

North Pole

SUN

Summer in the Northern Hemisphere

South Pole

THE MOVING LITHOSPHERE

THE EARTH'S LITHOSPHERE is broken up into 15 plates in which the continents are embedded. Some continents lie within a plate, while others have a plate boundary through them. Forces in the Earth's mantle move the plates slowly around the globe, a process called continental drift. Rift valleys, ocean trenches, and mountains have all formed in areas where plates meet.

The plates of the Earth's lithosphere fit together like a jigsaw puzzle

Hot rocky material circulates under the plates

PLATE MOVEMENT
Plates collide, overlap, and slide past each other as they move around the globe. When plates collide, one plate may be forced under another into the mantle to form a deep ocean trench, or push rock upward to form mountains.

220 MILLION YEARS AGO
Scientists believe that about 220 million years ago the world's continents were part of one giant continent called Pangaea. Over the following 20 million years, it split into Laurasia and Gondwanaland.

80 MILLION YEARS AGO
Africa and South America separated 180 million years ago, breaking away from Antarctica. The Atlantic Ocean was created by a spreading ridge between North America, Europe, and Africa.

PRESENT DAY
Scientists can only guess what the world was like before Pangaea, but if the movement of plates continues, the Great Rift Valley will become an island and Africa and Europe will fuse.

SLIDING PLATES
The San Andreas fault, where two plates are sliding past each other, extends for 600 miles (965 km) in California. Movement between the plates is not steady and pressure builds up, causing earthquakes. About 90 percent of earthquakes occur in the "Ring of Fire," around the Pacific plate.

CLIMATE AND VEGETATION

THE MAIN INFLUENCES on an area's climate are its distance from a large body of water, its height above sea level, and the amount of sunlight it receives. Rainfall and sunlight levels are highest at the equator where the habitats with the most plant and animal life are found: rainforests, mangrove swamps, and coral reefs.

POLAR
Polar regions are so cold that few plants can survive. The treeless tundra regions of Siberia, Canada, Scandinavia, and Alaska support moss and lichens, as well as small flowers and shrubs during summer.

COOL
Coastal areas have less extreme climates than inland regions. Coniferous forests grow in cold northern Asia and North America. Warmer areas have forests of deciduous trees, which lose their leaves in winter.

WARM
Hot, dry summers and wet winters are typical of the Mediterranean region as well as parts of Southern Africa, the Americas, and Australia. Vegetation varies from treeless grasslands to open forests of trees and shrubs.

The world's largest remaining rainforest is in the Amazon Basin, Brazil

DESERT AND DRY LANDS

Arid and semiarid lands cover more
[tha]n 30 percent of the Earth's land surface.
[A] semiarid region scattered with grasses and
[shr]ubs is called a savanna. Cold deserts, like
[th]e ice deserts of the Arctic and Antarctic,
[ha]ve no more rain than the Sahara.

TROPICAL

High temperatures and
high rainfall are typical of the
Tropics. The main difference
between tropical and monsoon
climates is the distribution of
rainfall. Tropical rainforests
near the equator depend on
year-round rainfall.

*The coniferous forests of
Asia and northernmost
Europe are called taiga*

MOUNTAIN

Vegetation on the
lower slopes depends on the
climate zone in which the
mountain is located.
Mountains become colder
with altitude and only
hardy alpine plants
grow above the
treeline. Snow and
bare rock occur
above the snowline.

TROPICAL MONSOON

Tropical regions with distinct
[w]et and dry seasons have a monsoon
[cli]mate. Each year, the monsoon winds
[re]verse their direction completely,
[fo]rming the two seasons.

*Gum trees, or
Eucalyptus,
have adapted to
dry conditions*

WORLD TIME ZONES

IMAGINARY LINES are drawn around the globe, either parallel to the equator (latitude) or from pole to pole (longitude, or meridians). The Earth is divided into 2 time zones, one for each hour of the day. Greenwich on 0° meridian and time advances by one hour for every 15° of longitude east of Greenwich.

TIME ZONES
The numbers on the map indicate the number of hours which must be subtracted or added to reach GMT. When it is noon at Greenwich, for example, it is 7 a.m. in New York City. Time zones are adjusted to regional administrative boundaries.

KEY TO MAP	
⬤	MINUS HOURS
⬤	PLUS HOURS
○	GREENWICH MEAN TIME
◐	DATE LINE
▮▮	TIME ZONES

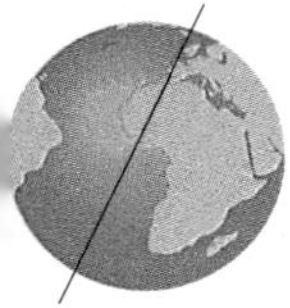

GMT
Greenwich Mean
Time (GMT) is the
time in Greenwich,
England. Clocks are
set depending on
whether they are east
or west of Greenwich.

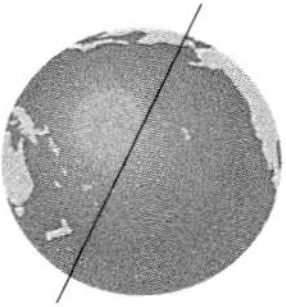

INTERNATIONAL DATE
LINE
The International
Date Line is an
imaginary line that
runs along the 180°
meridian but deviates
around countries.

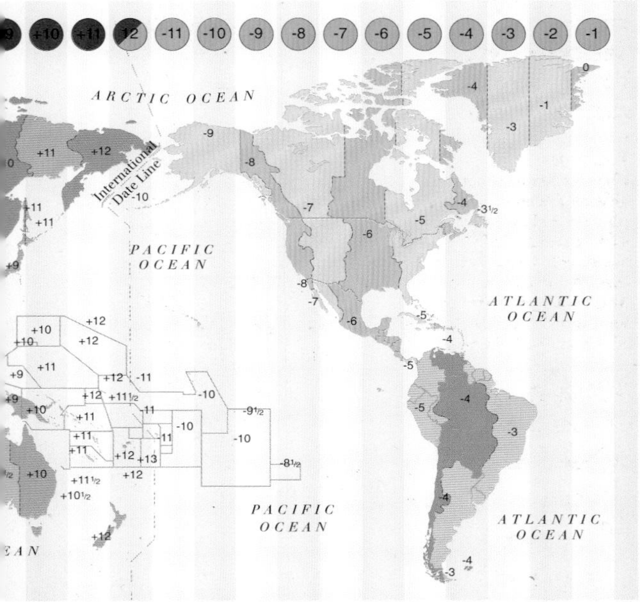

NORTH AMERICA

ARCTIC OCEAN

BEAUFORT SEA

Alaska

CANADA

GULF OF ALASKA

PACIFIC OCEAN

UNITED STATES

MEXICO

Hawaii

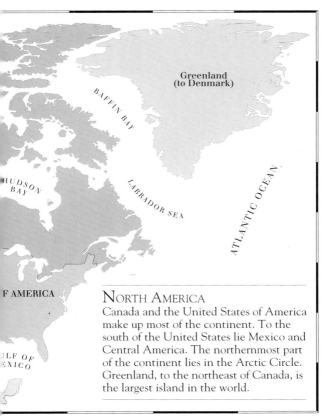

Greenland
(to Denmark)

BAFFIN BAY

HUDSON BAY

LABRADOR SEA

ATLANTIC OCEAN

F AMERICA

ULF OF
EXICO

NORTH AMERICA

Canada and the United States of America
make up most of the continent. To the
south of the United States lie Mexico and
Central America. The northernmost part
of the continent lies in the Arctic Circle.
Greenland, to the northeast of Canada, is
the largest island in the world.

ALASKA AND
WESTERN CANADA

AT THE END OF the last ice age, people traveled from Asia into North America over the Bering land bridge, which connected the continents at present-day Alaska.

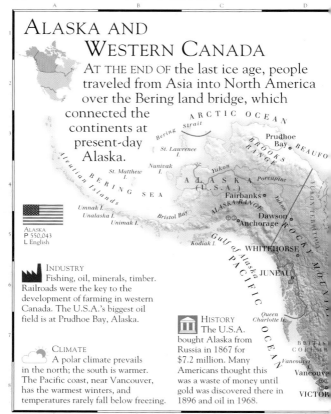

ARCTIC OCEAN

Bering Strait

St. Lawrence I.

Prudhoe Bay

BROOKS RANGE

BEAUFO

Nunivak I.

St. Matthew I.

Yukon

Porcupine

ALASKA (U.S.A.)

Fairbanks

YUKON TERRITORY

BERING SEA

Aleutian Islands

Umnak I.
Unalaska I.
Unimak I.

Bristol Bay

ALASKA RANGE

Dawson

Anchorage

Yukon

ROCKY MOUNTAINS

ALASKA
P 550,043
L English

Kodiak I.

Gulf of Alaska

WHITEHORSE

JUNEAU

PACIFIC

Queen Charlotte Is.

INDUSTRY
Fishing, oil, minerals, timber. Railroads were the key to the development of farming in western Canada. The U.S.A.'s biggest oil field is at Prudhoe Bay, Alaska.

HISTORY
The U.S.A. bought Alaska from Russia in 1867 for $7.2 million. Many Americans thought this was a waste of money until gold was discovered there in 1896 and oil in 1968.

OCEAN

BRITISH COLUMBIA

Vancouver I.

Vancouver

VICTOR

CLIMATE
A polar climate prevails in the north; the south is warmer. The Pacific coast, near Vancouver, has the warmest winters, and temperatures rarely fall below freezing.

A   B   C   D

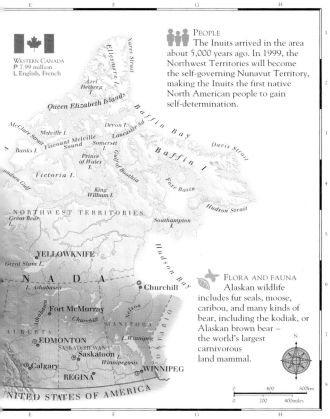

WESTERN CANADA
P 7.99 million
L English, French

PEOPLE
The Inuits arrived in the area about 5,000 years ago. In 1999, the Northwest Territories will become the self-governing Nunavut Territory, making the Inuits the first native North American people to gain self-determination.

FLORA AND FAUNA
Alaskan wildlife includes fur seals, moose, caribou, and many kinds of bear, including the kodiak, or Alaskan brown bear – the world's largest carnivorous land mammal.

Nares Strait
Ellesmere I.
Axel Heiberg I.
Queen Elizabeth Islands
Baffin Bay
McClure Strait
Melville I.
Devon I.
Lancaster Sd.
Davis Strait
Viscount Melville Sound
Somerset I.
Banks I.
Prince of Wales I.
Gulf of Boothia
Baffin I.
amundsen Gulf
Victoria I.
King William I.
Foxe Basin
NORTHWEST TERRITORIES
Great Bear L.
Hudson Strait
Southampton I.
YELLOWKNIFE
Hudson Bay
Great Slave L.
N   A   D   A
L. Athabasca
Churchill
Athabasca
Fort McMurray
Churchill
MANITOBA
ALBERTA
Nelson
ONTARIO
EDMONTON
SASKATCHEWAN
L. Winnipeg
Calgary
Saskatoon
Winnipegosis
REGINA
WINNIPEG
UNITED STATES OF AMERICA

N

0   400   800km
0   200   400miles

EASTERN CANADA

THE SECOND LARGEST country in the world, Canada has a relatively small population. Most people live within 100 miles (160 km) of the U.S.A. border. Snowbound for most of the year, the Hudson Bay area is a wilderness of forests, rivers, and lakes.

PEOPLE
The Vikings were the first Europeans to visit eastern Canada, in about 986 B.C. They settled for only a short time before Native Americans drove them away.

INDUSTRY
Wood industries, oil, zinc, nickel, hydroelectricity, uranium. The area off the east coast, called the Grand Banks, is one of the world's richest fishing areas. A major export from the Atlantic provinces is newsprint, made from wood pulp.

Salisbury
Nottingham I.
Mansel I.

Inukjuak

Hudson Bay

Belcher Is.

MANITOBA

C. Henrietta Maria

Severn

Winisk

James Bay

Attawapiskat
Attawapiskat

Albany

O N T A R I O

C A N A

Lake of the Woods

L. Nipigon

UNITED

Thunder Bay

Lake Superior

STATES

Sault Sainte Marie

Timmins

Ottawa

Sudbury

O F

Lake Huron

Lake Michigan

A M E R I C A

TORONTO
Lake Ontario

Hamilton

London

Niagara Falls

Windsor

L. Erie

UNITE

CLIMATE
January temperatures average below 0°F (–18°C) in more than two-thirds of Canada. Summers are short and cool in the north, but warm enough for farming in the south.

HISTORY
In the 15th and 16th centuries, two expeditions, from England and France, reached Canada and each claimed it. The struggle for territory led to war and France was forced to give up its territories to Great Britain in 1763.

COMMUNICATIONS
With the completion of the Canadian Pacific Railway in 1885, Canada's east and west coasts were linked for the first time. The country is so vast that there are five time zones within its borders.

EASTERN CANADA
P 19.3 million
L English, French

0   200   400km
0   100   200miles

NORTHEASTERN STATES

WITH ITS RICH MINERAL resources and safe harbors, the Northeast was the first area on the continent to be colonized by Europeans. In 1620, English pilgrims sailed on the *Mayflower* to settle in a region that is still called New England. During the mid-19th century, European immigrants settled in New York City and in other East Coast cities. Today, this region is the most densely populated and heavily industrialized area of the U.S.A.

CLIMATE

This area of the U.S.A has a temperate climate, with warm and humid summers. However, the northeastern region, in particular, can experience very heavy snowfall from November to April.

NORTHEASTERN STATES
P 51.5 million
L English

PEOPLE

Northeastern Native American tribes, such as the Wampanoag, the Algonquin, and the tribes of the Iroquois League, were the first to come into contact with European settlers and explorers.

INDUSTRY

Oil, iron, steel, chemicals, maple sugar, blueberries, cranberries, fishing, tourism. Vermont is the main producer of maple syrup in the U.S.A. The stock exchange on Wall Street, New York City, is the largest in the world.

Niag
Fr
Lake Erie Buff
Erie
OHIO
PENNSYLVAN
Pittsburgh
WEST
VIRGINIA
APPALACH
MTS

E   F   G   H

1

NATURAL FEATURES
Lying on the border
between the U.S.A. and Canada,
Niagara Falls were formed about
10,000 years ago. About 180,000
tons (tonnes) of water go over
the falls every minute.

2

C A N A D A

M A I N E

Moosehead L.

Champlain

3

ADIRONDACK MTS. **MONTPELIER** WHITE MTS.

Ontario

chester

Syracuse

Mohawk

AUGUSTA

CONCORD

4

HISTORY
In 1621, the
Mayflower pilgrims
celebrated their first
successful harvest.
Thanksgiving is now
an annual holiday,
observed on the
last Thursday
in November.

nger Lakes

ALBANY

N E W Y O R K

CATSKILL MTS.

MASSACHUSETTS **BOSTON**

Springfield Worcester *Cape Cod*

5

Susquehanna

Hudson

HARTFORD CONNECTICUT

PROVIDENCE RHODE ISLAND

Waterbury

New Haven

Nantucket I.

Martha's Vineyard

Paterson Bridgeport

Delaware

Allentown Newark New York City

Long I.

6

HARRISBURG **TRENTON**

Wilmington Philadelphia

MARYLAND Newark NEW JERSEY

A T L A N T I C   O C E A N

7

DOVER

DELAWARE

FLORA AND FAUNA
The Appalachian
Mountains are home to the
opossum, North America's
only species of marsupial,
or pouched mammal.

N

0   100   200km

0   50   100miles

8

E   F   G   H

SOUTHERN STATES

BY THE 19TH CENTURY, the wealth of the South was based on crops like tobacco, indigo, rice, and especially cotton, which was grown on large plantations by African slaves. The area is known today for New Orleans' jazz, Florida's Disney World, and the Kentucky Derby. The city of Washington, in the District of Columbia, was made the U.S. capital in 1800.

MISSOURI

BOSTON MTS.

OKLAHOMA

LITTLE ROCK   Memphis

ARKANSAS

Ouachita   Arkansas   Mississippi

TEXAS

Shreveport   Red R.

Yazoo

MISSISSIP

•JACKSO

LOUISIANA   Mississippi

BATON ROUGE ⊙ Pontchartrain

New   L.   Mobile
Orleans

Mississippi Delta

CLIMATE
Summers are long and hot; winters are mild, but temperatures are generally warmer on the coast than inland. Southern Florida is tropical.

INDUSTRY
Soybeans, coal, peanuts, cotton, citrus fruits, tobacco, oil, tourism. Georgia grows half of the U.S.A.'s peanuts – most are used to make peanut butter.

THE ARTS
The French brought Mardi Gras to America in the early 1700s. Celebrated in many of the southern states, the most famous festival is held in New Orleans, where parade last for a week before Mardi Gras Day, the day before Lent starts.

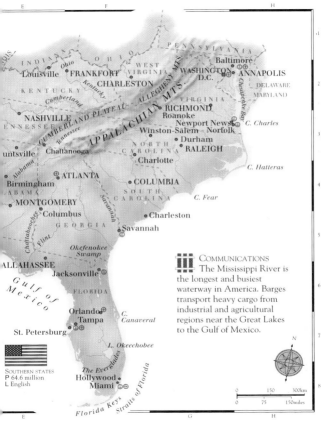

PENNSYLVANIA

INDIANA   OHIO

Louisville Ohio FRANKFORT WEST   WASHINGTON ANNAPOLIS
                               VIRGINIA   D.C.
            CHARLESTON   DELAWARE
KENTUCKY   Kentucky   MARYLAND
         Cumberland   VIRGINIA
NASHVILLE   RICHMOND
                      Roanoke
ENNESSEE   Tennessee   Newport News Norfolk C. Charles
                       Winston-Salem
untsville Chattanooga   Durham
                  NORTH   RALEIGH
                  CAROLINA
                  Charlotte
         ATLANTA   C. Hatteras
Birmingham   COLUMBIA
ABAMA   SOUTH
MONTGOMERY   CAROLINA   C. Fear
  Columbus
      GEORGIA   Savannah
                Charleston
          Savannah

          Okefenokee
          Swamp

ALLAHASSEE   **III** COMMUNICATIONS
  Jacksonville   The Mississippi River is
                                      the longest and busiest
Gulf of   waterway in America. Barges
Mexico   FLORIDA   transport heavy cargo from
                                      industrial and agricultural
                                      regions near the Great Lakes
     Orlando C.   to the Gulf of Mexico.
     Tampa   Canaveral
St. Petersburg   N

          L. Okeechobee

SOUTHERN STATES   The Everglades
P 64.6 million   Hollywood
L English   Miami   0   150   300km

          Florida Keys Straits of Florida   0   75   150miles

THE GREAT LAKES

THE STATES OF Indiana, Illinois, Michigan, Ohio, Wisconsin, and Minnesota, all of which border on one or more of the five Great Lakes, are often called the industrial and agricultural heartland of the United States. The region is rich in natural resources, with large areas of fertile farmland on flat plains called prairies.

Lake of the Woods

Upper Red L.

NORTH DAKOTA

Lower Red L.

Leech L.

MINNESOTA

SOUTH DAKOTA

Mississippi

Minneapol

ST PA

CLIMATE
The region around the Great Lakes has warm summers but quite severe winters, and parts of the lakes can freeze over. Minnesota, in particular, suffers from heavy snowstorms.

GREAT LAKES STATES
P 46.4 million
L English

ENVIRONMENT
The Great Lakes – Ontario, Huron, Superior, Michigan, and Erie – together form the largest area of freshwater in the world. Heavy industry has caused severe water pollution, and in some areas it is dangerous to eat the fish or swim.

INDUSTRY
Vehicles, coal, iron, grains, cherries. Nearly half of the world's corn crop and a third of the cherry crop are grown in the Great Lakes region. Detroit is known as "motor city" because it is the center of the U.S. car industry.

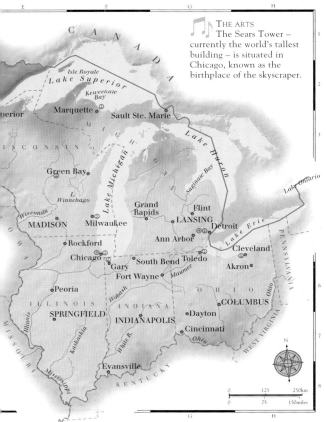

THE ARTS
The Sears Tower – currently the world's tallest building – is situated in Chicago, known as the birthplace of the skyscraper.

CANADA

Isle Royale

Lake Superior

Keweenaw Bay

Marquette

Sault Ste. Marie

Superior

WISCONSIN

Lake Huron

Saginaw Bay

Green Bay

Lake Michigan

L. Winnebago

Wisconsin

MADISON

Milwaukee

Rockford

Grand Rapids

Flint

LANSING

Detroit

Lake Ontario

Lake Erie

Cleveland

PENNSYLVANIA

Ann Arbor

Chicago

Gary

South Bend

Toledo

Akron

Fort Wayne

Maumee

Peoria

Wabash

ILLINOIS

INDIANA

OHIO

COLUMBUS

SPRINGFIELD

INDIANAPOLIS

Dayton

Cincinnati

White R.

Ohio

Illinois

Kaskaskia

MISSOURI

Mississippi

Evansville

KENTUCKY

WEST VIRGINIA

Ohio

N

0   125   250km
0   75   150miles

CENTRAL AND MOUNTAIN STATES

THE GREAT Plains, the Rocky Mountains, and the Mississippi lowlands dominate the landscape of the Midwest. Once home to Native Americans and herds of bison, the Great Plains were settled in the 19th century by Europeans, who forced the Native Americans onto reservations and slaughtered the bison to near-extinction.

HISTORY
Pioneers traveling to the West had to cross the Great Plains, which were known as the "Great American Desert." The last region to be settled, it is now a wealthy agricultural region.

CLIMATE
Summers are cooler and winters warmer than they are east of the Rockies. The Great Plains have an extreme climate, which can change quite suddenly and violently – blizzards, hail, thunderstorms, and tornadoes may occur.

CENTRAL AND
MOUNTAIN STATES
P 18.7 million
L English

NATURAL FEATURES
The Rocky Mountains exten through Canada and the U.S.A. fo more than 3,000 miles (4,800 km). Dividing North America, they separate the rivers flowing west to the Pacific from those flowing east to the Atlantic.

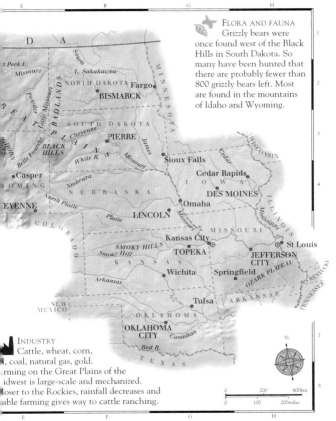

FLORA AND FAUNA
Grizzly bears were once found west of the Black Hills in South Dakota. So many have been hunted that there are probably fewer than 800 grizzly bears left. Most are found in the mountains of Idaho and Wyoming.

INDUSTRY
Cattle, wheat, corn, ..., coal, natural gas, gold. ...rming on the Great Plains of the ...idwest is large-scale and mechanized. ...oser to the Rockies, rainfall decreases and ...able farming gives way to cattle ranching.

D   A
t Peck L.
Missouri
Souris
L. Sakakawea
NORTH DAKOTA   Fargo
BISMARCK
MINNESOTA
Powder
Little Missouri
BADLANDS
GREAT PLAINS
SOUTH DAKOTA
Belle Fourche
BLACK HILLS
Cheyenne
PIERRE
James
Casper
White R.
Missouri
Sioux Falls
WISCONSIN
YOMING
Niobrara
NEBRASKA
Cedar
Cedar Rapids
IOWA
North Platte
DES MOINES
ILLINOIS
EYENNE
Platte
LINCOLN
Omaha
Missouri
COLORADO
Mississippi
SMOKY HILLS
Smoky Hill
Kansas City
MISSOURI
St Louis
TOPEKA
JEFFERSON CITY
KANSAS
Wichita
Springfield
KENTUCKY
Arkansas
OZARK PLATEAU
NEW MEXICO
Tulsa
ARKANSAS
TENNESSEE
OKLAHOMA
OKLAHOMA CITY
Canadian
Red R.
TEXAS

N

0   200   400km
0   100   200miles

E   F   G   H

SOUTHWESTERN STATES

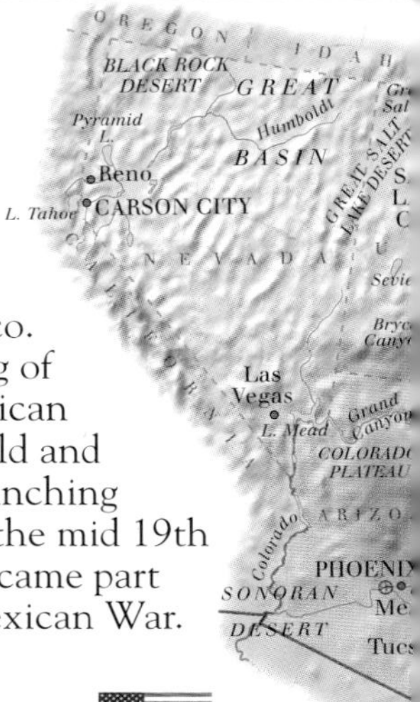

THE FIRST Europeans in the Southwest were the Spanish, who traveled north from Mexico. This resulted in a mingling of Spanish and Native American cultures in this region. Gold and silver mining and cattle-ranching attracted other settlers in the mid 19th century, when this area became part of the U.S.A. after the Mexican War.

Map labels: OREGON, IDAHO, BLACK ROCK DESERT, GREAT, Pyramid L., Humboldt, BASIN, GREAT SALT LAKE DESERT, Reno, CARSON CITY, L. Tahoe, NEVADA, SLC, Sevier, Bryce Canyon, Las Vegas, L. Mead, Grand Canyon, COLORADO PLATEAU, Colorado, ARIZONA, PHOENIX, SONORAN DESERT, Me, Tucs, Gt Salt

NATURAL FEATURES
The Colorado plateau has some unusual landforms, including natural bridges and arches of solid rock. Over the last million years, the Colorado River has cut away the plateau, forming the world's largest river gorge – the Grand Canyon.

SOUTHWESTERN STATES
P 28.4 million
L English

PEOPLE
Some of the earliest Native Americans lived in the Nevada area. Bones and ashes discovered near Las Vegas indicate that they may have lived there more than 20,000 years ago. Today, the region has the largest concentration of Native Americans in the country.

HISTORY
At the end of the Mexican War (1846–48), the U.S.A. acquired Utah, Nevada, California, and parts of Arizona, New Mexico, Colorado, and Wyoming. One of the causes of the war was a border dispute between Texas and Mexico.

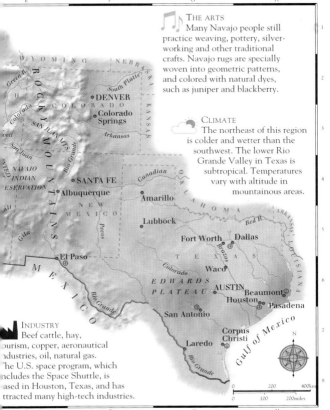

THE ARTS
Many Navajo people still practice weaving, pottery, silver-working and other traditional crafts. Navajo rugs are specially woven into geometric patterns, and colored with natural dyes, such as juniper and blackberry.

CLIMATE
The northeast of this region is colder and wetter than the southwest. The lower Rio Grande Valley in Texas is subtropical. Temperatures vary with altitude in mountainous areas.

INDUSTRY
Beef cattle, hay, tourism, copper, aeronautical industries, oil, natural gas. The U.S. space program, which includes the Space Shuttle, is based in Houston, Texas, and has attracted many high-tech industries.

WYOMING
NEBRASKA
Green R.
ROCKY MOUNTAINS
Colorado
SAN JUAN MTS
DENVER
COLORADO
Colorado Springs
South Platte
KANSAS
Arkansas
San Juan
Rio Grande
Gila
NAVAJO INDIAN RESERVATION
SANTA FE
Albuquerque
NEW MEXICO
Canadian
OKLAHOMA
Amarillo
Pecos
Lubbock
Red R.
ARKANSAS
LOUISIANA
El Paso
MEXICO
Rio Grande
Colorado
Brazos
Fort Worth
Dallas
TEXAS
Waco
EDWARDS PLATEAU
AUSTIN
Beaumont
Houston
Pasadena
San Antonio
Corpus Christi
Laredo
Rio Grande
Gulf of Mexico

N

0   200   400km
0   100   200miles

PACIFIC STATES

ALL THREE STATES on the West Coast are major agricultural producers – Washington and Oregon supply one-third of the softwood timber for the U.S.A., and California produces half of the country's fruit and vegetables. Situated where two of the Earth's plates meet, the area suffers from earthquakes and volcanic activity. Mount St. Helens, dormant since 1857, erupted in 1980, losing some 1,300 ft (400 m) off its height.

NATURAL FEATURES
The lowest point in the western hemisphere is in Death Valley, 282 ft (86 m) below sea level. One of the driest, hottest places on Earth, the highest temperature, 135°F (57°C), was recorded there in 1913, and its average rainfall is only 1.5 in (38 mm) per year.

Franklin D. Roosevelt L.

Banks L.

Columbia

Spokane

CANADA

WASHINGTON

Walla Walla

Baker City

BLUE MOUNTAINS

Snake

Yakima

Columbia

OREGON

Everett

Bellevue

Seattle

Tacoma

San Juan Is.

Strait of Juan de Fuca

OLYMPIA

Portland

SALEM

Newport

Eugene

CASCADE RANGE

OCEAN

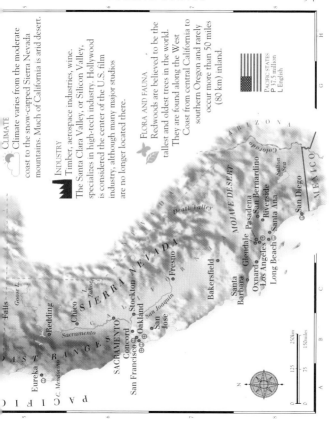

CLIMATE

Climate varies from the moderate coast to the snow-capped Sierra Nevada mountains. Much of California is arid desert.

INDUSTRY

Timber, aerospace industries, wine. The Santa Clara Valley, or Silicon Valley, specializes in high-tech industry. Hollywood is considered the center of the U.S. film industry, although many major studios are no longer located there.

FLORA AND FAUNA

Redwoods are believed to be the tallest and oldest trees in the world. They are found along the West Coast from central California to southern Oregon and rarely occur more than 50 miles (80 km) inland.

PACIFIC STATES
P 37.5 million
L English

MEXICO

THE ANCIENT empires of the Maya and Aztec flourished for centuries before the Spanish invaded Mexico in 1519, lured there by legends of hoards of gold and silver. Mexico gained its independence in 1836, after 300 years of Spanish rule. Today, most Mexicans are *mestizo*, a mix of Spanish and Native American. Although Spanish is the official language, Native American languages such as Maya, Nahuatl, and Zapotec are also widely spoken.

CLIMATE
The Mexican plateau and mountains are warm for most of the year. The Pacific coast has a tropical climate.

Mexico
P 84.4 million
L Spanish

FLORA AND FAUNA
The Mexican beaded lizard and the gila monster are the only two poisonous lizards known. The largest of all cacti is the giant saguaro, which grows in the Sonora Desert to a height of more than 60 ft (18 m).

NATURAL FEATURES
The plateau of Mexico is enclosed to the west and east by the Sierra Madre mountain ranges, which occupy 75 percent of the total land area. Mexico is so mountainous and arid in parts that only 12 percent of the land is arable

E   F   G   H

ENVIRONMENT
Poor air quality is a problem in Mexico City because it is surrounded by mountains, which stop fumes released by cars and factories from escaping.

HISTORY
The remains of Mayan and Aztec cities are found all over Mexico and Central America. Mexico City is built on the ruins of the Aztec capital, Tenochtitlán.

INDUSTRY
Oil, natural gas, tourism, minerals, brewing, agriculture. Tourism employs nine percent of the workforce. Mexico is one of the largest oil producers and supplies one-fifth of the world's silver.

F A M E R I C A

Ciudad Juárez

Bravo del Norte

Chihuahua

Río Grande

nchos

M E X I C O

SIERRA MADRE ORIENTAL

Monterrey

OCCIDENTAL

San Luis Potosí

Río Grande de Santiago

ías

Aguascalientes

Ciudad Madero

L. Chapala

León

Guadalajara

Poza Rica

Mérida

Gulf of Mexico

Campeche

Cozumel I.

YUCATÁN PENINSULA

MEXICO CITY Texcoco
Puebla

Bay of Campeche

Balsas

SIERRA MADRE DEL SUR

Villahermosa

BELIZE

Acapulco

Coatzacoalcos

Oaxaca

Tuxtla Gutiérrez

P A C I F I C   O C E A N

N

Gulf of Tehuantepec

Tapachula

GUATEMALA

200   400km

100   200miles

E   F   G   H

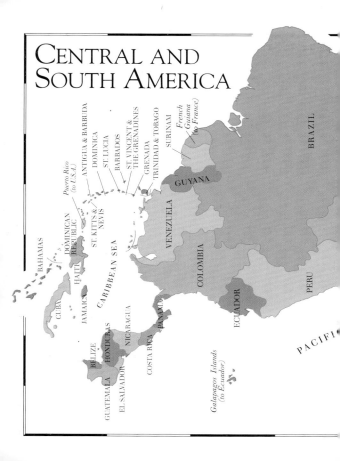

CENTRAL AND SOUTH AMERICA

BAHAMAS

CUBA

HAITI

DOMINICAN REPUBLIC

Puerto Rico
(to U.S.A.)

ANTIGUA & BARBUDA

DOMINICA

ST. LUCIA

BARBADOS

ST. VINCENT &
THE GRENADINES

GRENADA

TRINIDAD & TOBAGO

ST. KITTS &
NEVIS

JAMAICA

CARIBBEAN SEA

SURINAM

French
Guiana
(to France)

GUYANA

VENEZUELA

COLOMBIA

BRAZIL

PERU

ECUADOR

BELIZE

GUATEMALA

EL SALVADOR

HONDURAS

NICARAGUA

COSTA RICA

PANAMA

Galapagos Islands
(to Ecuador)

PACIFIC

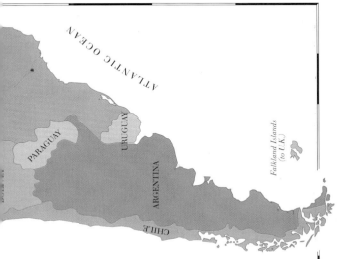

ATLANTIC OCEAN

PARAGUAY

URUGUAY

ARGENTINA

CHILE

Falkland Islands
(to U.K.)

OCEAN

CENTRAL AND SOUTH AMERICA

Until three million years ago, South America was an island with its own unique flora and fauna. The narrow Isthmus of Panama is the continent's only link to North America. South America's southernmost tip, Cape Horn, is only 600 miles (970 km) from Antarctica.

CENTRAL AMERICA AND THE CARIBBEAN

CENTRAL AMERICA FORMS a narrow land bridge joining North and South America. To the east lie the Caribbean islands, many of which are uninhabited.

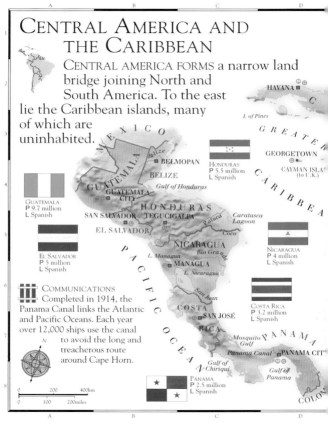

HAVANA

I. of Pines

GREATER

GEORGETOWN

CAYMAN ISLANDS
(to U.K.)

CARIBBEAN

MEXICO

BELMOPAN

BELIZE

Gulf of Honduras

HONDURAS
P 5.5 million
L Spanish

GUATEMALA
CITY

GUATEMALA
P 9.7 million
L Spanish

SAN SALVADOR

HONDURAS

TEGUCIGALPA

Patuca

Caratasca
Lagoon

Coco

EL SALVADOR

EL SALVADOR
P 5 million
L Spanish

NICARAGUA

Río Grande

L. Managua

NICARAGUA
P 4 million
L Spanish

MANAGUA

L. Nicaragua

San Juan

COMMUNICATIONS

Completed in 1914, the Panama Canal links the Atlantic and Pacific Oceans. Each year over 12,000 ships use the canal to avoid the long and treacherous route around Cape Horn.

COSTA

SAN JOSÉ

COSTA RICA
P 3.2 million
L Spanish

RICA

PACIFIC OCEAN

Mosquito
Gulf

PANAMA

Panama Canal

PANAMA CITY

Gulf of
Chiriquí

Gulf of
Panama

COLO

N

0   200   400km
0   100   200miles

PANAMA
P 2.5 million
L Spanish

ATLANTIC OCEAN

Great Bahama Bank

NASSAU

BAHAMAS

GRAND TURK

TURKS & CAICOS ISLANDS (to U.K.)

CUBA
P 10.8 million
L Spanish

BAHAMAS
P 264,000
L English

CLIMATE
Although most of this region has a tropical climate, which is generally hot and humid all year, mountain and highland areas are cooler and drier.

INDUSTRY
Sugar, coffee, bananas. Bananas are exported from many Central American countries on refrigerated cargo ships, and are also used to make a local beer.

DOMINICAN REPUBLIC
P 7.3 million
L Spanish

JAMAICA
KINGSTON

HAITI

Windward Passage

PORT-AU-PRINCE

DOMINICAN REPUBLIC

SANTO DOMINGO

SEA

ANTILLES

SAN JUAN
PUERTO RICO
(to U.S.A.)

LEEWARD ISLANDS

VIRGIN ISLANDS
(to U.S.A.)

BRITISH VIRGIN ISLANDS
(to U.K.)

ANGUILLA
(to U.K.)

ANTIGUA & BARBUDA

JAMAICA
P 2.5 million
L English

HAITI
P 6.8 million
L French, French Creole

ST. KITTS & NEVIS

MONTSERRAT (to U.K.)

GUADELOUPE
(to France)

DOMINICA

MARTINIQUE
(to France)

ST. LUCIA

LESSER ANTILLES

WINDWARD ISLANDS

HISTORY
The thousands of islands in the Caribbean were originally called the West Indies because European explorers thought they were part of India.

LESSER ANTILLES

ARUBA
(to Neth.)

NETHERLANDS ANTILLES

ST. VINCENT & THE GRENADINES

GRENADA

BARBADOS

TRINIDAD & TOBAGO

Tobago

TRINIDAD AND TOBAGO
P 1.3 million
L English

PORT OF SPAIN

VENEZUELA

Trinidad

E F G H

NORTHERN SOUTH AMERICA

THE INCAS RULED MUCH of this area in the 15th century, and today large numbers of their descendants live in Peru, Ecuador, and Bolivia. In 1533, the last Incan emperor was executed by the Spanish, who colonized this region. Countries east of Venezuela were later settled by the French, Dutch, and British, although all but French Guiana are now independent.

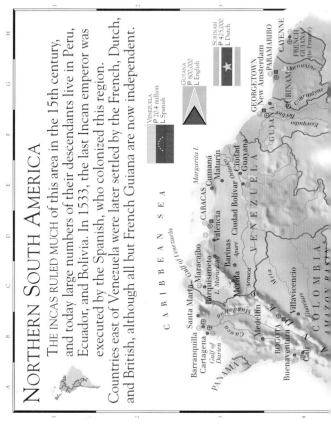

VENEZUELA
P 20.4 million
L Spanish

GUYANA
P 800,000
L English

SURINAM
P 425,000
L Dutch

CARIBBEAN   SEA

Gulf of Venezuela

Margarita I.

Barranquilla
Cartagena   Santa Marta
Gulf of Darién   Maracaibo   Barquisimeto
L. Maracaibo   Valencia   CARACAS   Cumaná   Maturín
PANAMA   Mérida   Barinas   Ciudad   Ciudad Bolívar   Guayana
Medellín   Apure   Guárico   Orinoco
Buenaventura   Meta   VENEZUELA
Cali   BOGOTA   Villavicencio   Arauca
COLOMBIA   Guaviare
Cauca   Magdalena   GUYANA

GEORGETOWN
New Amsterdam
PARAMARIBO   CAYENNE
SURINAM   FRENCH GUIANA
(to France)

Essequibo   Berbice
Corantyne   Maroni/Marowijne

AMAZON BASIN

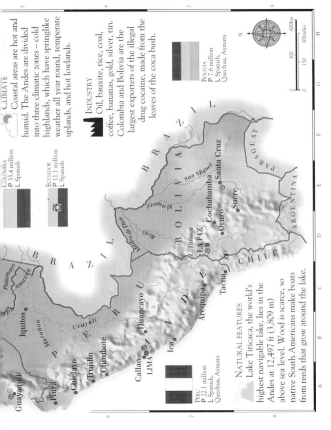

CLIMATE
Coastal areas are hot and humid. The Andes are divided into three climatic zones – cold highlands, which have springlike weather all year round, temperate uplands, and hot lowlands.

INDUSTRY
Oil, bauxite, rice, coal, coffee, bananas, gold, silver, tin. Colombia and Bolivia are the largest exporters of the illegal drug cocaine, made from the leaves of the coca bush.

BOLIVIA
P 7.6 million
L Spanish,
Quechua, Aymara

COLOMBIA
P 33.4 million
L Spanish

ECUADOR
P 11.1 million
L Spanish

NATURAL FEATURES
Lake Titicaca, the world's highest navigable lake, lies in the Andes at 12,497 ft (3,809 m) above sea level. Wood is scarce, so native South Americans make boats from reeds that grow around the lake.

PERU
P 22.1 million
L Spanish,
Quechua, Aymara

BRAZIL

OCCUPYING NEARLY HALF of South America, Brazil has the largest river basin in the world. Many Brazilians are descendants of Portuguese, who colonized Brazil in the 16th century and Africans, who were brought to work on sugar plantations. Brazil's Native American tribes have little contact with the outside world. In 1992, the United Nations held its first Earth Summit in Rio, partly to highlight the destruction of the Amazon rainforest, the largest rainforest in the world.

PEOPLE

There were once about two million indigenous people living in Amazonia. Today only 50,000 remain. The survival of many tribes and their way of life is threatened by the destruction of the Amazon rainforest.

ATLANTIC OCEAN

Fortaleza

Teresina

São Luís

Belém

SERRA PELADA

FRENCH GUIANA (to France)

SURINAM

GUYANA

VENEZUELA

COLOMBIA

Xingu

Santarém

Amazon

Tapajós

Manaus

Balbina Res.

Negro

Madeira

Purus

Amazon

AMAZON BASIN

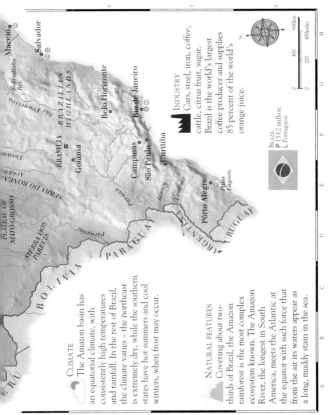

CLIMATE
The Amazon basin has an equatorial climate, with consistently high temperatures and rainfall. In the rest of Brazil, the climate varies – the northeast is extremely dry, while the southern states have hot summers and cool winters, when frost may occur.

NATURAL FEATURES
Covering about two-thirds of Brazil, the Amazon rainforest is the most complex ecosystem known. The Amazon River, the longest in South America, meets the Atlantic at the equator with such force that from the air its waters appear as a long, muddy stain in the sea.

INDUSTRY
Cars, steel, iron, coffee, cattle, citrus fruit, sugar. Brazil is the world's largest coffee producer and supplies 85 percent of the world's orange juice.

BRAZIL
P 153.2 million
L Portuguese

0   400   800km
0   200   400miles

Maceió
Salvador
obradinho
Res.
São Francisco
BRAZILIAN
HIGHLANDS
Belo Horizonte
Rio de Janeiro
BRASÍLIA
Goiânia
Campinas
São Paulo
Curitiba
Tocantins
Araguaia
SERRA DO RONCA
PLATEAU OF
MATO GROSSO
SIERRA DOS
PARECIS
Paraguay
Paraná
Iguaçu
Uruguay
Patos
Lagoon
Pôrto Alegre
BOLIVIA
PARAGUAY
ARGENTINA
URUGUAY
PERU

N

A   B   C   D   E   F   G   H

SOUTHERN SOUTH AMERICA

THE LANDSCAPE OF this region of South America varies from snow-capped volcanoes in the Andes to the wastelands of Patagonia. In the heart of Argentina lie the Pampas, fertile grasslands where vast herds of cattle graze. In parts, grasses grow up to 10 ft (3 m) high. Chile is separated from the rest of the region by the Andes, which run the length of the continent.

CLIMATE

Paraguay is subtropical, farther south is temperate. The Andes have snow year-round, while parts of the Atacama desert in Chile have had no rain for 400 years.

PARAGUAY
P 4.5 million
L Spanish,
Guaraní

URUGUAY
P 3.1 million

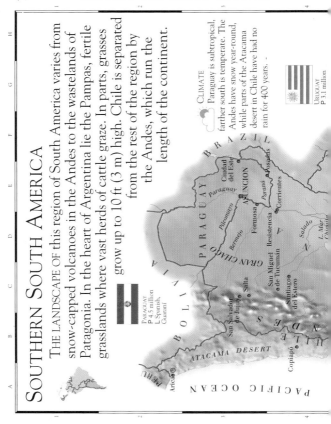

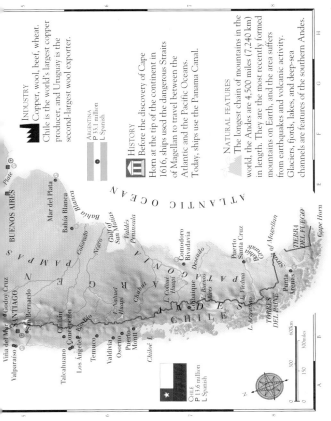

INDUSTRY
Copper, wool, beef, wheat. Chile is the world's largest copper producer, and Uruguay is the second-largest wool exporter.

ARGENTINA
P 33.1 million
L Spanish

HISTORY
Before the discovery of Cape Horn at the tip of the continent in 1616, ships used the dangerous Straits of Magellan to travel between the Atlantic and the Pacific Oceans. Today, ships use the Panama Canal.

NATURAL FEATURES
The longest chain of mountains in the world, the Andes are 4,500 miles (7,240 km) in length. They are the most recently formed mountains on Earth, and the area suffers from earthquakes and volcanic activity. Glaciers, fjords, lakes, and deep-sea channels are features of the southern Andes.

ATLANTIC OCEAN

BUENOS AIRES
Plata
Mar del Plata
Bahía Blanca
Colorado
Negro
Gulf of San Matías
Valdés Peninsula
P A M P A S
PATAGONIA
Chubut
Commodoro Rivadavia
Deseado
Puerto Santa Cruz
Río Santa Cruz
Río Gallegos
Strait of Magellan
TIERRA DEL FUEGO
Cape Horn

SANTIAGO
Godoy Cruz
San Bernardo
Viña del Mar
Valparaíso
Chillán
Talcahuano
Concepción
Los Ángeles
Bío Bío
Temuco
Valdivia
Osorno
Puerto Montt
Chiloé I.
L. Nahuel Huapi
L. Colhué Huapi
Cohaique
L. Buenos Aires
L. Viedma
L. Argentino
TORRES DEL PAINE
Punta Arenas
A N D E S
C H I L E

CHILE
P 13.6 million
L Spanish

N

600 km
300
100 miles
150
0

THE ANTARCTIC

CONTAINING 80 PERCENT of the world's freshwater, the continent of Antarctica lies buried under ice more than 1.2 miles (2 km) thick. The surrounding seas are partly frozen, and icebergs barricade over 9 percent of the coastline.

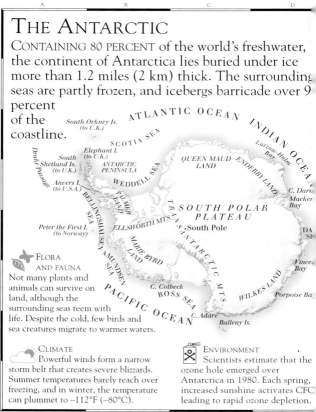

South Orkney Is.
(to U.K.)

ATLANTIC OCEAN

INDIAN OCEA

SCOTIA SEA

Elephant I.
(to U.K.)

South
Shetland Is.
(to U.K.)

ANTARCTIC
PENINSULA

QUEEN MAUD
LAND

Lützow-Holm
Bay

ENDERBY LAND

Drake Passage

Anvers I.
(to U.S.A.)

WEDDELL SEA

PALMER
LAND

C. Darl
Macker
Bay

SOUTH POLAR
PLATEAU

BELLINGSHAUSEN
SEA

ELLSWORTH MTS.

Peter the First I.
(to Norway)

•South Pole

DA
SI

TRANSANTARCTIC MTS.

MARIE BYRD
LAND

AMUNDSEN
SEA

Vince
Bay

PACIFIC OCEAN

C. Colbeck
ROSS SEA

WILKES LAND

Porpoise Ba

C. Adare

Balleny Is.

FLORA
AND FAUNA
Not many plants and animals can survive on land, although the surrounding seas teem with life. Despite the cold, few birds and sea creatures migrate to warmer waters.

CLIMATE
Powerful winds form a narrow storm belt that creates severe blizzards. Summer temperatures barely reach over freezing, and in winter, the temperature can plummet to –112°F (–80°C).

ENVIRONMENT
Scientists estimate that the ozone hole emerged over Antarctica in 1980. Each spring, increased sunshine activates CFC leading to rapid ozone depletion.

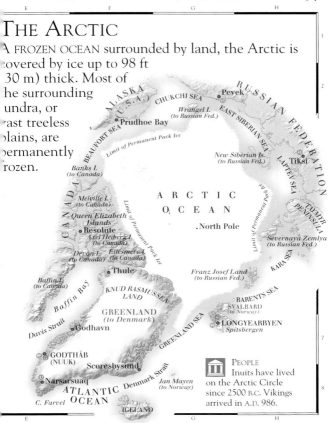

THE ARCTIC

A FROZEN OCEAN surrounded by land, the Arctic is
covered by ice up to 98 ft
(30 m) thick. Most of
the surrounding
tundra, or
vast treeless
plains, are
permanently
frozen.

ALASKA
(U.S.A.)
CHUKCHI SEA
Pevek
RUSSIAN FEDERATION
Wrangel I.
(to Russian Fed.)
BEAUFORT SEA
Prudhoe Bay
EAST SIBERIAN SEA
Limit of Permanent Pack Ice
New Siberian Is.
(to Russian Fed.)
Tiksi
LAPTEV SEA
Banks I.
(to Canada)

CANADA

Melville I.
(to Canada)
Queen Elizabeth
Islands
Resolute
Axel Heiberg I.
(to Canada)
Devon I.
(to Canada)
Ellesmere I.
(to Canada)
Thule

ARCTIC
OCEAN

North Pole

TAYMYR PENINSULA

Severnaya Zemlya
(to Russian Fed.)

Limit of Permanent Pack Ice

Baffin I.
(to Canada)
Baffin Bay

KNUD RASMUSSEN
LAND

Franz Josef Land
(to Russian Fed.)

KARA SEA

Davis Strait
Godhavn

GREENLAND
(to Denmark)

BARENTS SEA
SVALBARD
(to Norway)
LONGYEARBYEN
Spitsbergen

GREENLAND SEA

GODTHÅB
(NUUK)

Scoresbysund

Narsarsuaq

Denmark Strait

Jan Mayen
(to Norway)

ATLANTIC
OCEAN
C. Farvel

ICELAND

PEOPLE
Inuits have lived
on the Arctic Circle
since 2500 B.C. Vikings
arrived in A.D. 986.

E   F   G   H

ATLANTIC OCEAN

BENEATH THE WATERS of the Atlantic Ocean lies the Mid-Atlantic Ridge, one of the world's longest mountain chains. Some of its peaks are so high they form islands, such as the Azores. Apart from a wide rift-valley in the center of the ridge, the ocean consists of vast featureless plains and is 5 miles (8 km) at its deepest point.

ICELAND
P 270,000
L Icelandic

CAPE VERDE
P 390,000
L Portuguese

EUROPE

Murmansk

Bergen

Rotterdam

BALTIC SEA

NORTH SEA

Aberdeen

BLACK SEA

MEDITERRANEAN SEA

GIBRALTAR

ARCTIC OCEAN

GREENLAND SEA

GREENLAND

ICELAND
REYKJAVIK

Faeroe Islands
(to Denmark)

Denmark Strait

Jan Mayen

Azores
(to Portugal)

Madeira
(to Portugal)

Mid-Atlantic Ridge

Baffin Bay

Davis Strait

LABRADOR SEA

Cape Farewell

Newfoundland

Grand Banks

A

Bermuda
(to U.K.)

Hudson Bay

St. Lawrence

New York
City

NORTH AMERICA

Mississippi

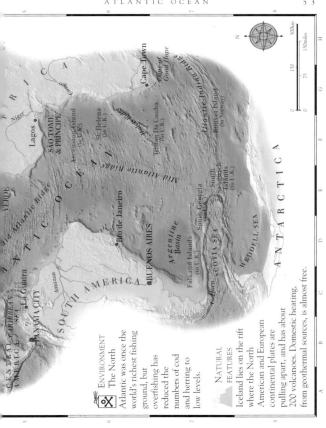

N

0   150   300km
0   75   150miles

AFRICA

Congo

Niger

Lagos

SÃO TOMÉ & PRÍNCIPE

Ascension Island (to U.K.)

St. Helena (to U.K.)

Tristan Da Cunha (to U.K.)

Cape Town

Cape of Good Hope

Bouvet Island (to Norway)

Walvis Ridge

Mid-Atlantic Ridge

ATLANTIC OCEAN

VERDE

Mid Atlantic Ridge

Amazon

SOUTH AMERICA

Rio de Janeiro

BUENOS AIRES

Argentine Basin

Falkland Islands (to U.K.)

C. Horn

SCOTIA SEA

South Georgia (to U.K.)

South Sandwich Islands (to U.K.)

WEDDELL SEA

ANTARCTICA

CARIBBEAN SEA

La Guaira

PANAMA CITY

ENVIRONMENT

The North Atlantic was once the world's richest fishing ground, but overfishing has reduced the numbers of cod and herring to low levels.

NATURAL FEATURES

Iceland lies on the rift where the North American and European continental plates are pulling apart, and has about 200 volcanoes. Domestic heating, from geothermal sources, is almost free.

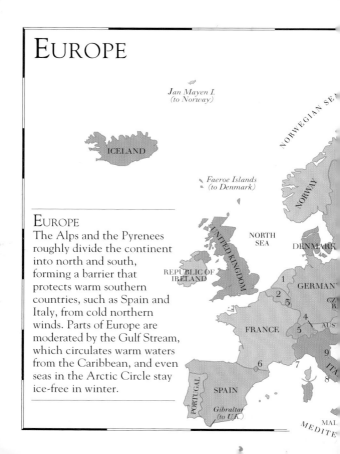

EUROPE

Jan Mayen I.
(to Norway)

ICELAND

NORWEGIAN SE

Faeroe Islands
(to Denmark)

NORWAY

EUROPE

The Alps and the Pyrenees
roughly divide the continent
into north and south,
forming a barrier that
protects warm southern
countries, such as Spain and
Italy, from cold northern
winds. Parts of Europe are
moderated by the Gulf Stream,
which circulates warm waters
from the Caribbean, and even
seas in the Arctic Circle stay
ice-free in winter.

NORTH
SEA

UNITED KINGDOM

REPUBLIC OF
IRELAND

DENMARK

GERMAN

CZ
R

1
2
3
4
AUS
5

FRANCE

9

ITA

6
7
8

PORTUGAL

SPAIN

Gibraltar
(to U.K.)

MAL

MEDITE

BARENTS SEA

FINLAND

ESTONIA

BALTIC SEA

LATVIA

LITHUANIA

RUSSIAN
FEDERATION

BELARUS

LAND

OVAKIA

NGARY

UKRAINE

16

ROMANIA

13

BULGARIA

BLACK SEA

GEORGIA

AZERBAIJAN

ARMENIA

14

15

GREECE

NEAN SEA

1 NETHERLANDS
2 BELGIUM
3 LUXEMBOURG
4 LIECHTENSTEIN
5 SWITZERLAND
6 ANDORRA
7 MONACO
8 VATICAN CITY
9 SAN MARINO
10 SLOVENIA
11 CROATIA
12 BOSNIA/HERZEGOVINA
13 YUGOSLAVIA
14 MACEDONIA
15 ALBANIA
16 MOLDOVA

SCANDINAVIA AND FINLAND

DURING PAST ICE AGES, much of Scandinavia and Finland were covered in glaciers that carved out the land, leaving steep-sided valleys, fjords, and lakes. The Finns, originally from the east via Russia, differ from Scandinavians in culture and language.

CLIMATE
Norway's west coast is warmed by the Gulf Stream. Northern temperatures fall to −22°F (−30°C) during the six-month winter; the south is milder.

INDUSTRY
Fishing, timber, wood-pulp, paper, oil, gas, car manufacture. Norway is western Europe's largest producer of oil.

NORWAY
P 4.3 million
L Norwegian

FINLAND
P 5 million
L Finnish,
Swedish

RUSSIAN FEDERATION

ARCTIC OCEAN

North Cape

Hammerfest

L. Inari

Ounas

F I N L

Oulu

Oulu

Torne

L. Oulu

Tornio

L. Päijänne

Tromsø

L. Inni

NORWEGIAN SEA

Lofoten Vesteralen

North Cape

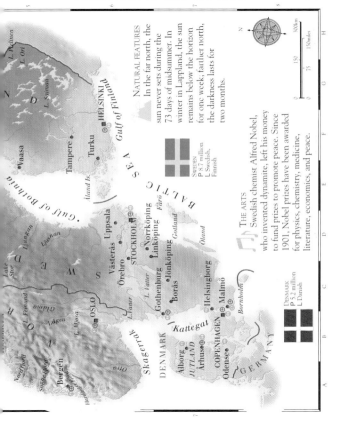

NATURAL FEATURES
In the far north, the sun never sets during the 73 days of midsummer. In winter in Lapland, the sun remains below the horizon for one week; farther north, the darkness lasts for two months.

SWEDEN
P. 8.7 million
L. Swedish, Finnish

THE ARTS
Swedish chemist Alfred Nobel, who invented dynamite, left his money to fund prizes to promote peace. Since 1901, Nobel prizes have been awarded for physics, chemistry, medicine, literature, economics, and peace.

DENMARK
P. 5.2 million
L. Danish

THE BRITISH ISLES

LYING OFF THE COAST of mainland Europe, the British Isles consist of two main islands, Ireland and Great Britain, and many smaller islands. England, Scotland, Wales, and Northern Ireland form the United Kingdom (U.K.). The Republic of Ireland became independent of the U.K. in 1921.

UNITED KINGDOM
P 58 million
L English

NATURAL FEATURES
The highest point in the British Isles is Ben Nevis in Scotland, at a height of 4,406 ft (1 343 m)

Shetland Is.

Orkney Is.

NORTH SEA

Aberdeen

GRAMPIAN MTS.

HIGHLANDS

SCOTLAND

Ben Nevis

Forth

Tay

Edinburgh

Glasgow

Lomond

SOUTHERN UPLANDS

Outer Hebrides

Lewis

North Uist

South Uist

Barra

Skye

Coll

Tiree

Mull

Colonsay

Jura

Islay

Arran

Kintyre

Londonderry

ATLANTIC OCEAN

NORTH SEA

UNITED KINGDOM

Isle of Man
(to U.K.)

PENNINES
LAKE
DISTRICT

Tees

Kingston
upon Hull

Leeds

Bradford Sheffield
Manchester

Liverpool Nottingham
Stoke-on-Trent Trent
Derby Leicester
Wolverhampton Birmingham
Coventry

ENGLAND

CAMBRIAN MTS.

Anglesey

IRELAND

IRISH SEA

DUBLIN

Liffey

Galway
Shannon
Barrow
Blackwater
Cork
Shannon

**BRECON
BEACONS**

Cardiff

EXMOOR

DARTMOOR

Plymouth

Isle of
Scilly

Bristol

Severn

Thames

LONDON

Southampton

Isle of Wight

English Channel

Channel Is.

Guernsey (to U.K.)

*Jersey
(to U.K.)*

IRELAND
P 3.5 million
L Irish, English

☁ **CLIMATE**
Warmed by the Gulf
Stream, the climate is mild
but changeable. Rainfall
is well distributed
throughout the year.

🏭 **INDUSTRY**
Pharmaceuticals, aerospace industry, oil, natural
gas, dairy products, computer parts, livestock.
Ireland has one of Europe's fastest growing economies.

N

200km
100miles
0 50 100

SPAIN AND PORTUGAL

SUPREME SKILL IN shipbuilding and navigation enabled both Spain and Portugal to become the most powerful empires of the 16th century. Both have a seafaring history; Christopher Columbus sailed to America in 1492, and Vasco da Gama, the Portuguese explorer, was the first to sail around Africa to India in 1497.

INDUSTRY

Fishing, car manufacture, olives, cork, ship building, citrus fruit, tourism. Spain and Portugal are famous for fortified wines. Sherry is named after Jerez de la Frontera, Spain, and Port after Porto, Portugal.

CLIMATE

Spain's coastal areas are milder than the central plateau, which has a more extreme temperature range. Almeria, Spain, contains Europe's only desert. Portugal's Mediterranean-like climate is moderated by the Atlantic.

ATLANTIC OCEAN

Oviedo

Santiago de Compostela

Galicia

Minho

Esla Res.

Porto

Douro

Coimbra

Tagus

Alcántara Res.

LISBON

Setúbal

Guadiana

Beja

SIERR

Lagos

Sevilla

Faro

PORTUGAL
P 9.9 million
L Portuguese

Gibraltar
GIBRALTA
(to U.K.)

Strait o

E F G H

SPAIN
P 39.1 million
L Spanish, Galician, Basque, Catalan

Bay of Biscay
⊕ Santander

Basque provinces
Vitoria • Pamplona

Logroño •

F R A N C E

P Y R E N E E S

ANDORRA

Catalonia

alladolid *Duero*

Zaragoza •
Ebro

Barcelona ⊕ ⊞

A I N

Mequinenza
Res.

RA DE GUADARRAMA

⊕⊞ MADRID

• Toledo

us

Valencia

Valencia ⊕ ⊞
Júcar

Baleric Islands

Minorca

Majorca
• Palma de
⊕ Mallorca

Ibiza

Guadiana

RENA
alquivir

Segura

SIERRA DE SEGURA

• Murcia

M E D I T E R R A N E A N   S E A

dalusia

SIERRA NEVADA

• Málaga
⊕⊞

raltar

N

0   100   200km
0   50   100miles

PEOPLE
The Spanish are fiercely regional and each province has its own language and literature – Catalonia, Galicia, and the Basque Provinces are the largest. The Basques, who live in the Pyrenees, now have their own parliament.

E F G H

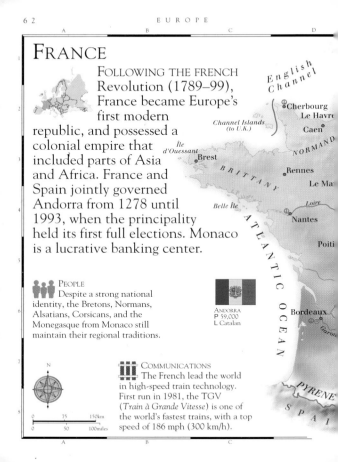

FRANCE

FOLLOWING THE FRENCH Revolution (1789–99), France became Europe's first modern republic, and possessed a colonial empire that included parts of Asia and Africa. France and Spain jointly governed Andorra from 1278 until 1993, when the principality held its first full elections. Monaco is a lucrative banking center.

PEOPLE
Despite a strong national identity, the Bretons, Normans, Alsatians, Corsicans, and the Monegasque from Monaco still maintain their regional traditions.

ANDORRA
P 59,000
L Catalan

COMMUNICATIONS
The French lead the world in high-speed train technology. First run in 1981, the TGV (*Train à Grande Vitesse*) is one of the world's fastest trains, with a top speed of 186 mph (300 km/h).

English Channel

Cherbourg
Le Havre
Channel Islands
(to U.K.)
Caen

NORMAND

Île d'Ouessant
Brest

BRITTANY

Rennes
Le Ma

Belle Île

Loire
Nantes

Poiti

ATLANTIC OCEAN

Bordeaux
Garon

PYRENE

SPAI

N

0   75   150km
0   50   100miles

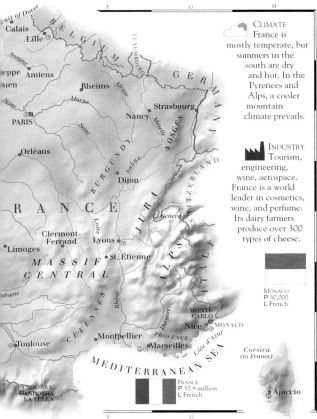

Strait of Dover

Calais
Lille

Somme

eppe Amiens

uen

Seine

PARIS

Orléans

Limoges

dogne

Toulouse

ANDORRA
ANDORRA
LA VELLA

BELGIUM

LUXEMBOURG

GERMANY

Rheims

Meuse

Marne

Nancy Strasbourg

Moselle

Seine

VOSGES

BURGUNDY

Dijon

Saône

JURA

SWITZERLAND

L. Geneva

Clermont-
Ferrand   Lyons

Loire

St. Étienne

MASSIF
CENTRAL

Rhône

ALPS

ITALY

CÉVENNES

Durance

MONTE
CARLO

Montpellier PROVENCE Nice MONACO

Marseilles *Côte d'Azur*

MEDITERRANEAN SEA

F R A N C E

Corsica
(to France)

Ajaccio

☁ CLIMATE
France is
mostly temperate, but
summers in the
south are dry
and hot. In the
Pyrenees and
Alps, a cooler
mountain
climate prevails.

🏭 INDUSTRY
Tourism,
engineering,
wine, aerospace.
France is a world
leader in cosmetics,
wine, and perfume.
Its dairy farmers
produce over 300
types of cheese.

MONACO
P 30,000
L French

FRANCE
P 57.8 million
L French

THE LOW COUNTRIES

BELGIUM, THE NETHERLANDS, and
Luxembourg are known as the
"Low Countries"
because they are flat
and low-lying. Much of the
Netherlands lies below sea
level and has been
reclaimed from the sea.
The Low Countries, also
called "Benelux," are
Europe's most densely
populated countries.

CLIMATE

The region is mostly
temperate. Coastal areas
are mildest, warmed by
the Gulf Stream.
Luxembourg's
winters are cold
and snowy.

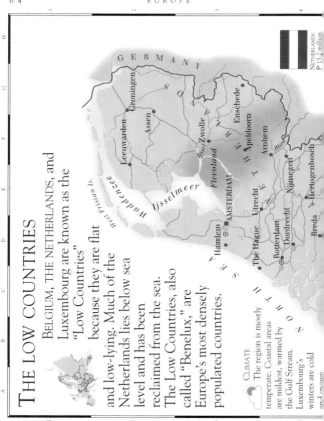

GERMANY

NETHERLANDS
P 15.2 million

Groningen

Leeuwarden

Assen

West Frisian Is.

Waddenzee

IJsselmeer

Zwolle

IJssel

Flevoland

Enschede

Apeldoorn

Arnhem

Rhine

Nijmegen

's-Hertogenbosch

Haarlem

AMSTERDAM

Utrecht

The Hague

Rotterdam

Dordrecht

Breda

NORTH SEA

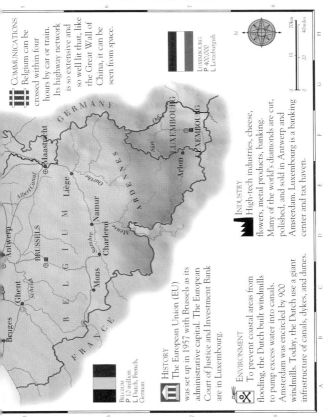

COMMUNICATIONS
Belgium can be crossed within four hours by car or train. Its highway network is so extensive and so well lit that, like the Great Wall of China, it can be seen from space.

LUXEMBOURG
P 400,000
L Letzeburgish

N

0   15   70km
0   20   40miles

HISTORY
The European Union (EU) was set up in 1957 with Brussels as its administrative capital. The European Court of Justice and Investment Bank are in Luxembourg.

ENVIRONMENT
To prevent coastal areas from flooding, the Dutch built windmills to pump excess water into canals. Amsterdam was encircled by 900 windmills. Today, the Dutch use a giant infrastructure of canals, dykes, and dunes.

INDUSTRY
High-tech industries, cheese, flowers, metal products, banking. Many of the world's diamonds are cut, polished, and sold in Antwerp and Amsterdam. Luxembourg is a banking center and tax haven.

BELGIUM
P 10 million
L Dutch, French, German

GERMANY

Maastricht

ARDENNES

LUXEMBOURG

LUXEMBOURG

Arlon

Sûre

Our

Albert Canal

Liège

Ourthe

Namur

Meuse

Charleroi

Sambre

BELGIUM

Antwerp

BRUSSELS

Ghent

Schelde

Mons

Bruges

FRANCE

GERMANY

IT WAS NOT UNTIL 1871 that many small independent states were united under Prussia to form Germany. After 1945, the country was divided again, into a democratic West Germany and a Soviet-dominated East Germany. Reunified in 1990, Germany is, like France, a leading member of the European Union and is currently Europe's strongest economic power.

INDUSTRY
Cars, heavy and precision engineering, electronics, chemicals. Germany has a strong industrial sector and is Europe's main car producer.

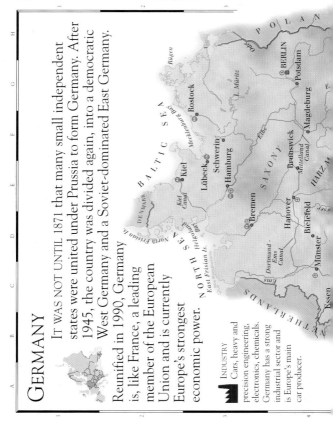

N

0 40 80miles
0 75 150km

BELGIUM
LUXEMBOURG
FRANCE
SWITZERLAND
AUSTRIA
CZECH REPUBLIC
ORE MTS.

Aachen • Bonn
Cologne
Wiesbaden
Mainz
Saarbrücken
Frankfurt
Mannheim
Karlsruhe
Stuttgart
Nuremberg
Augsburg
Munich
Erfurt
Chemnitz

RHINELAND

Rhine
Moselle
Main
Neckar
Danube
Danube
L. Constance

Thuringian Forest
Black Forest
FRANCONIAN JURA
SWABIAN JURA
BAVARIA
BAVARIAN ALPS

GERMANY
P 80.3 million
L German

CLIMATE

The Rhine
Valley is mild and is
suitable for wine-making.
The Bavarian Alps and
Black Forest are much
colder, with heavy
snowfalls in winter.

HISTORY

After World War II,
Berlin was shared among the
Allies. In 1955, Berlin was
divided between East and West
Germany. The Berlin Wall was
built in 1961 to prevent people
from defecting to the West.

ENVIRONMENT

Germany has strict pollution controls,
recycling most paper, glass, and used tires.
Acid rain is damaging many of Germany's
forests and the Rhine is heavily polluted
by industry.

SWITZERLAND AND AUSTRIA

ONCE THE CENTER OF the vast Hapsburg
Empire, the Republic of Austria was
created after World War I. Switzerland
has been a neutral country since 1815,
and many international organizations such as the
Red Cross have their headquarters there.
Liechtenstein is closely allied to
Switzerland, which handles
its foreign relations.

LIECHTENSTEIN
P 30,000
L German

SWITZERLAND
P 6.9 million
L German,
French, Italian

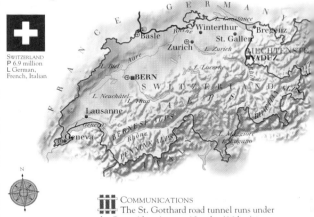

COMMUNICATIONS
The St. Gotthard road tunnel runs under
the Swiss Alps. At over 10 miles (16 km) in
length, it is the world's longest road tunnel.

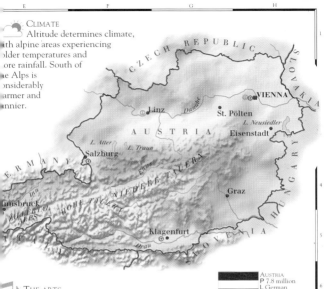

CLIMATE
Altitude determines climate, with alpine areas experiencing colder temperatures and more rainfall. South of the Alps is considerably warmer and sunnier.

THE ARTS
Many famous musicians, such as Beethoven, Mozart, Schubert, and Brahms, lived and worked in Vienna.

NATURAL FEATURES
The Alps form part of an almost continuous mountain-belt, stretching from the Pyrenees in France to the Himalayas in Asia. They are also the source of Europe's largest rivers – the Rhine, Rhône, and Danube.

AUSTRIA
P 7.8 million
L German

INDUSTRY
Pharmaceuticals, financial services, tourism, chemicals, electrical engineering. Liechtenstein is the center of world dental manufacture. False teeth and dental materials are exported to over 100 countries.

CENTRAL EUROPE

HISTORICALLY ONE OF the most unstable parts of the continent, central Europe became part of the Eastern Bloc after World War II. Czechoslovakia, Poland, and Hungary all had communist governments with strong ties with the former U.S.S.R. In 1989, they broke away from the Soviet Union and in 1993 Czechoslovakia split into the Czech Republic and Slovakia.

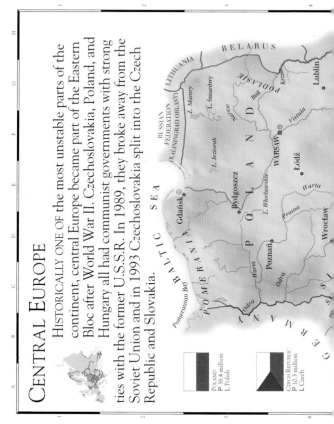

POLAND
P 38.4 million
L Polish

CZECH REPUBLIC
P 10.3 million
L Czech

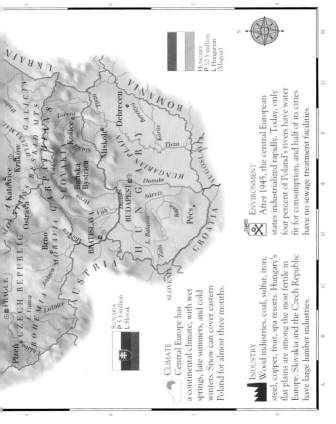

HUNGARY
P 10.5 million
L Hungarian
(Magyar)

SLOVAKIA
P 5.3 million
L Slovak

CLIMATE

Central Europe has a continental climate, with wet springs, late summers, and cold winters. Snow can cover eastern Poland for almost three months.

INDUSTRY

Wood industries, coal, sulfur, iron, steel, copper, fruit, spa resorts. Hungary's flat plains are among the most fertile in Europe. Slovakia and the Czech Republic have large lumber industries.

ENVIRONMENT

After 1945, the central European states industrialized rapidly. Today, only four percent of Poland's rivers have water fit for consumption, and half of its cities have no sewage treatment facilities.

ITALY AND MALTA

THE BOOT-SHAPED PENINSULA of Italy stretches from the Alps to the Ionian Sea and includes Sardinia, Sicily, and other small, offshore islands. Italy also contains two independent enclaves – the Vatican City in Rome and the Republic of San Marino near Rimini. The Romans, Arabs, French, Turks, Spanish, and British have all fought for or colonized Malta, which has been independent since 1964.

PEOPLE

Venetians were a seafaring people, whose ships carried silks and spices from Asia. The Venetian trader and explorer Marco Polo is said to have brought the recipe for pasta from China.

HISTORY

Italy was once a collection of small kingdoms and city-states, which were vulnerable to internal wars. It was united in 1870, through the efforts of the soldier Guiseppe Garibaldi and the politician

Count Camillo di Cavour

SLOVENIA

Trieste

Gulf of Venice

Venice

Mestre

Padua

Comacchio Lagoon

SAN MARINO

SAN MARINO

A D R I A T I

Verona

Po

Piave

Milan

L. Maggiore

L. Garda

Adige

Bologna

Arno

A P E N N I N E S

Turin

Genoa

Florence

Arno

Gulf of Genoa

LIGURIAN SE

L O M B A R D Y

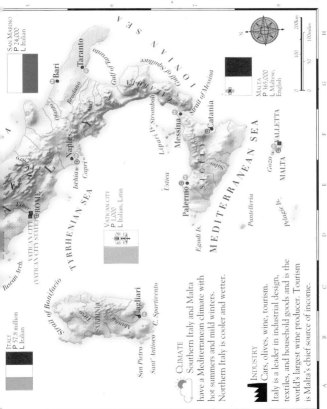

SAN MARINO
P 24,000
L Italian

IONIAN SEA

Taranto

Bari

Bradano

Ofanto

Agri

Gulf of Taranto

Gulf of Squillace

N

200km

100miles

100

50

0

0

MALTA
P 365,000
L Maltese,
English

CALABRIA

Sele

Naples

Lipari (S. Stromboli)

Messina

Strait of Messina

Catania

Ischia

Capri

SICILY

VALLETTA

Ofanto

Ustica

Egesi

Gozo

MALTA

Palermo

VATICAN CITY
P 1,000
L Italian, Latin

Tiber

VATICAN CITY
(VATICAN CITY STATE)

ROME

Tuscan Arch.

TYRRHENIAN SEA

Pantelleria

Pelagie Is.

MEDITERRANEAN SEA

ITALY
P 57.8 million
L Italian

Strait of Bonifacio

SARDINIA

Cagliari

Tirso

Mannu

C. Spartivento

San Pietro

Sant' Antioco

CLIMATE

Southern Italy and Malta have a Mediterranean climate with hot summers and mild winters. Northern Italy is cooler and wetter.

INDUSTRY

Cars, olives, wine, tourism. Italy is a leader in industrial design, textiles, and household goods and is the world's largest wine producer. Tourism is Malta's chief source of income.

| A | B | C | D | E | F | G |

THE WESTERN BALKANS

THE COUNTRIES OF Slovenia, Croatia, Dalmatia, Serbia, Montenegro, and Bosnia and Herzegovina were first united in 1918 and were named Yugoslavia in 1929. In 1991, civil war broke out between the main ethnic groups (Serbs, Muslims, Croats), resulting in the dissolution in 1992 of communist Yugoslavia. Serbia and Montenegro have since formed the Federal Republic of Yugoslavia, but warfare continues in Bosnia.

SLOVENIA
P 2 million
L Slovene

INDUSTRY
Coal, chromium, mercury ore.
UN sanctions against Yugoslavia and
war in Bosnia have taken a toll
on their economies.

YUGOSLAVIA
P 10.5 million
L Serbo-Croatian

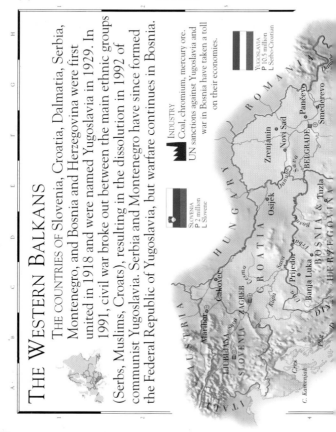

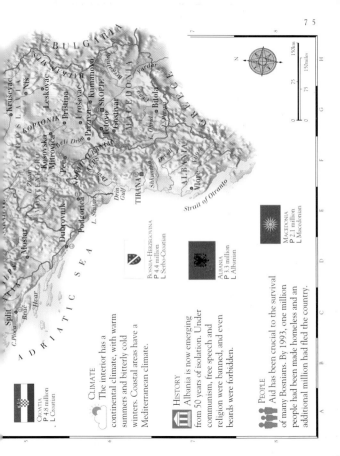

N

0   75   150km

0   75   150miles

CROATIA
P 4.8 million
L Croatian

BOSNIA-HERZEGOVINA
P 4.4 million
L Serbo-Croatian

ALBANIA
P 3.3 million
L Albanian

MACEDONIA
P 2.1 million
L Macedonian

CLIMATE

The interior has a continental climate, with warm summers and bitterly cold winters. Coastal areas have a Mediterranean climate.

HISTORY

Albania is now emerging from 50 years of isolation. Under communism, free speech and religion were banned, and even beards were forbidden.

PEOPLE

Aid has been crucial to the survival of many Bosnians. By 1993, one million people had been made homeless and an additional million had fled the country.

ROMANIA AND BULGARIA

AFTER A LONG history of invasion and occupation, Romania and Bulgaria became part of the Soviet bloc after World War II. In the early 1990s Romania and Bulgaria rose up against their repressive communist governments; Bulgaria's president was imprisoned and Romania's was executed.

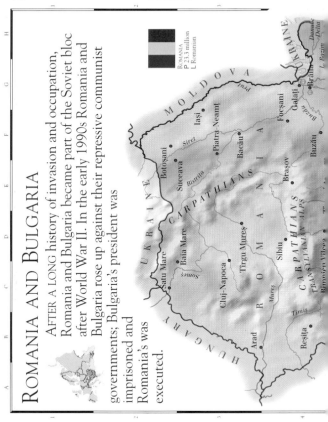

ROMANIA
P 23.3 million
L Romanian

UKRAINE

MOLDOVA

Prut

Iasi

Botoşani

Suceava

Satu Mare

Baia Mare

Someş

Cluj-Napoca

Tîrgu Mureş

Mureş

Sibiu

CARPATHIANS

TRANSYLVANIAN ALPS

Rîmnicu Vîlcea

Timiş

Arad

Reşiţa

HUNGARY

R O M A N I A

Bistriţa

Siret

Piatra-Neamţ

Bacău

Braşov

Buzău

Focşani

Galaţi

Buzău

Brăila

Danube

Delta

L Razim

UKRAINE

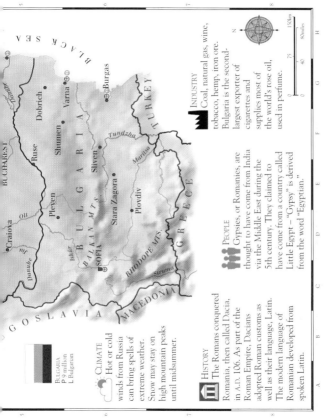

INDUSTRY

Coal, natural gas, wine, tobacco, hemp, iron ore. Bulgaria is the second-largest exporter of cigarettes and supplies most of the world's rose oil, used in perfume.

PEOPLE

Gypsies, or Romanies, are thought to have come from India via the Middle East during the 5th century. They claimed to have come from a country called Little Egypt – "Gypsy" is derived from the word "Egyptian."

CLIMATE

Hot or cold winds from Russia can bring spells of extreme weather. Snow may stay on high mountain peaks until midsummer.

HISTORY

The Romans conquered Romania, then called Dacia, in A.D. 106. As part of the Roman Empire, Dacians adopted Roman customs as well as their language, Latin. The modern language of Romanian developed from spoken Latin.

BULGARIA
P 9 million
L Bulgarian

GREECE

SURROUNDED BY THE Aegean,
Ionian, and Cretan seas, no
part of Greece is more than
85 miles (137 km)
from the coast. Its territory
includes the mainland on the
Balkan peninsula, and over
1,400 islands. The country is
mountainous and less than one-
third of the land is cultivated.
Greece gained its independence in
1830 after a long and fierce war,
ending 400 years of Turkish rule.

CLIMATE
Northwestern Greece is alpine,
while parts of Crete are almost
subtropical. The islands and the large
central plain of the mainland have
a Mediterranean climate, with high
summer temperatures and mild winters.

GREECE
P 10.3 million
L Greek

ENVIRONMENT
Athens suffers from smog, known
as *nefos*, which damages its ancient
monuments. The Parthenon, on the
Acropolis, has suffered more erosion
in the previous two decades than in the
previous two thousand years.

HISTORY
Regarded as the founders of
democracy, the ancient Greeks
were advanced for their time.
They were the first to study
medicine, geometry, and physics
(on a scientific basis), and Greece
was home to great thinkers such as
Plato, Aristotle, and Socrates.

MAC
Prest
Aliakm
ALBANIA
Corfu
Corfu
PINDUS MTS
Levkas
L. Trikhonis
Kefallinia
Gulf of Patrai
Pa
Zakinthos
IONIAN SEA

BULGARIA

THRACE

TURKEY

Thasos

Thessaloniki

Samothraki

Thermaic
Gulf

Limnos

arisa

Sporades

Skiros

Lesvos

Evvoia

Chios

A E G E A N   S E A

ATHENS

Andros

Samos

Piraeus

Kea

Cyclades

Kithnos

Serifos   Paros

Naxos

Kos

Sifnos

Milos

Ios

Rhodes

Dodecanese

Kithira

Thira

Rhodes

S E A   O F   C R E T E

Karpathos

M E D I T E R R A N E A N   S E A

Iraklion

Crete

INDUSTRY
Tourism, olives, fishing, citrus fruit, currants, sultanas, wine. Greece owns the world's largest shipping fleet and is one of Europe's major tourist spots. Olives and olive oil are major exports.

COMMUNICATIONS
Boats, ferries, and hydrofoils are commonly used for travel between the islands and the mainland. Greece has 444 ports; 123 handle heavy passenger and freight traffic. Piraeus is the country's main port.

N

0   100   200km

0   50   100miles

E   F   G   H

THE BALTIC STATES AND BELARUS

LITHUANIA, ESTONIA, AND LATVIA – the three Baltic States – were the first republics to declare their independence from the Soviet Union in 1990-91. Economic reform has been slow and problems still remain. Many areas of Belarus are still affected by the 1986 Chernobyl nuclear disaster. The cleanup will take decades, and is a major drain on the nation's finances.

PEOPLE
Russians, Belarussians, and Ukrainians resettled in Latvia when it was part of the U.S.S.R. Today Latvians make up only about half of the whole population, and they are a minority in the capital.

ESTONIA
P 1.6 million
L Estonian

LATVIA
P 2.7 million
L Latvian

BELARUS
P 10.3 million
L Belorussian

LITHUANIA
P 3.8 million
L Lithuanian

Gulf of Finland

RUSSIA

DAUGAVA

TALLINN

L. Peipus

Tartu

ESTONIA

Pärnu

Võrtsjärv

Hiiumaa

Saaremaa

RIGA

Gulf of Riga

Venta

Baltic

Sea

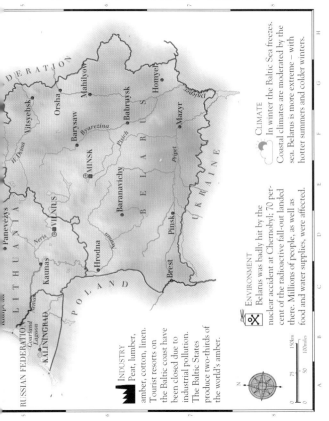

CLIMATE

In winter the Baltic Sea freezes. Coastal climates are moderated by the sea. Belarus is more extreme – with hotter summers and colder winters.

ENVIRONMENT

Belarus was badly hit by the nuclear accident at Chernobyl; 70 percent of the radioactive fall-out landed there. Millions of people, as well as food and water supplies, were affected.

INDUSTRY

Peat, lumber, amber, cotton, linen. Tourist resorts on the Baltic coast have been closed due to industrial pollution. The Baltic States produce two-thirds of the world's amber.

EUROPEAN RUSSIA

SPANNING THE TWO continents of Europe and Asia, the Russian Federation is the world's largest country. In 1917 the world's first communist government took power, and in 1923 Russia became the U.S.S.R., which included many territories that were once part of the Russian Empire. Economic reforms in the 1980s led to changes that resulted in the fall of communism in 1991.

INDUSTRY

Oil, gas, gold, diamonds, hydrocarbons, precious metals. Russia has large reserves of iron, coal, and nickel. Huge factories, which have grown without environmental controls, are causing pollution problems.

Novaya Zemlya

KARA SEA

Kara Vaygach I.

Spid

Vorkuta

BARENTS SEA

Kolguyev I.

Usa

Pechora

Murmansk

L.Imandra

KOLA PENINSULA

Arkhangel'sk

L.Pyaozero

L.Topozero

WHITE SEA

L.Segozero

Dvina

L.Onega

L.Ladoga

FINLAND

St. Petersburg

ESTONIA

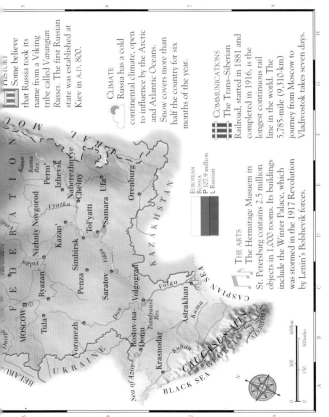

HISTORY
Some believe that Russia took its name from a Viking tribe called *Varangian Russes*. The first Russian state was established at Kiev in A.D. 800.

CLIMATE
Russia has a cold continental climate, open to influence by the Arctic and Atlantic Oceans. Snow covers more than half the country for six months of the year.

COMMUNICATIONS
The Trans-Siberian Railroad, started in 1881 and completed in 1916, is the longest continuous rail line in the world. The 5,785-mile (9,310-km) journey from Moscow to Vladivostok takes seven days.

EUROPEAN
RUSSIA
P 107.9 million
L Russian

THE ARTS
The Hermitage Museum in St. Petersburg contains 2.5 million objects in 1,000 rooms. Its buildings include the Winter Palace, which was stormed in the 1917 Revolution by Lenin's Bolshevik forces.

UKRAINE AND
THE CAUCASUS

SEPARATED FROM
the Russian
Federation by the Caucasus
mountains, the newly
independent Caucasian
Republics – Armenia,
Azerbaijan, and
Georgia – are rich in
natural resources. The
Ukraine, Europe's largest country, is
dominated by a flat and fertile plain.

ENVIRONMENT
As a result of the 1986 Chernobyl
nuclear disaster, 4 million Ukrainians
live in radioactive areas. In 1994,
reactors from the Chernobyl plant were
still being used to provide nuclear power.

CLIMATE
The Ukraine and
Moldova have a continental
climate, with distinctive
seasons. Armenia,
Azerbaijan, and Georgia
are protected from cold
air from the north by the
Caucasus mountains.

MOLDOVA
P 4.4 million
L Romanian

INDUSTRY
Coal, iron, cars, wine
citrus fruit, cotton, mineral
The Ukraine was known as
the breadbasket of the Sov
Union because its flat stepp
were extensively cultivated
Georgia's known oil reserve
are as yet unexploited.

N

0   150   300km
0   75   150miles

Map labels: BELARUS, POLAND, SLOVAKIA, HUNGARY, ROMANIA, MOLDOVA, U K R, Luts'k, Rivne, L'viv, Ternopil', Khmel'nyts'kyy, Ivano-Frankivs'k, Chernivtsi, Chernobyl, Kiev Res., KIEV, Zhytomyr, Bila Tserkva, Vinnytsya, Chisina, Mykol, Odesa, Desna, Styr, Sluch, Dniester, Prut

UKRAINE
P 52 million
L Ukrainian

PEOPLE
There are about 40 languages and 150 dialects spoken in the Caucasian republics. No relationship has yet been established between languages spoken within the Caucasus and those outside it.

NATURAL FEATURES
The Caucasus mountains extend for 750 miles (1,200 km). They form a natural boundary between Europe and Asia, and separate temperate climate zones from warmer areas.

FLORA AND FAUNA
The Russian sturgeon grows up to 23 ft (7m) long. Its eggs, called caviar, are a delicacy, but numbers of sturgeon are falling owing to polluted water.

GEORGIA
P 5.5 million
L Georgian

AZERBAIJAN
P 7.2 million
L Azerbaijani

HISTORY
With its strategic position, the Crimean peninsula has had a troubled history. It was part of Greece until 100 B.C., Turkey from 1475, and Russia from 1783, and was the scene of the Crimean War in 1853-56.

ARMENIA
P 3.5 million
L Armenian

Sumy
Kharkiv
menchuk
Kramators'k
nipropetrovs'k   Horlivka   Luhans'k
vvy Rih   Donets'k   Makiyivka
Dnieper   Zaporizhzhya
Kakhovka Res.
rson   Mariupol'
SEA OF AZOV
Kerch Strait
IMEA   Simferopol'
Sevastopol'
BLACK SEA
RUSSIAN FEDERATION
CAUCASUS
GEORGIA   MTS.
K'ut'aisi   TBILISI
Gyumri   Vanadzor   Ganca
ARMENIA   YEREVAN
AZERBAIJAN   BAKU
CASPIAN SEA
Kura
DONBASS
RUSSIAN FEDERATION

AFRICA

RED SEA

MEDITERRANEAN SEA

ERITREA
DJIBOUTI
ETHIOPIA

EGYPT
SUDAN
CENTRAL

LIBYA
CHAD

TUNISIA
NIGER

ALGERIA
MALI

MOROCCO

NIGERIA
BENIN
TOGO
GHANA
BURKINA
FASO
COTE
D'IVOIRE

Madeira
(to Portugal)
Canary Islands
(to Spain)

WESTERN
SAHARA

MAURITANIA
SENEGAL
GAMBIA
GUINEA-BISSAU
GUINEA
SIERRA
LEONE

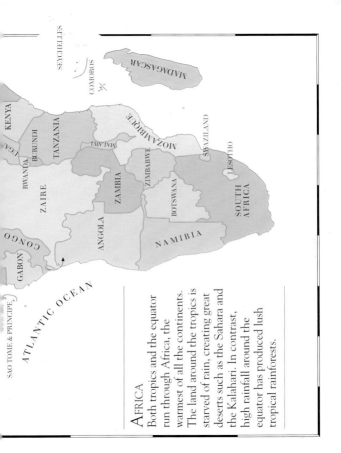

SEYCHELLES

COMOROS

MADAGASCAR

KENYA

...GA

RWANDA

BURUNDI

TANZANIA

ZAIRE

MALAWI

MOZAMBIQUE

ZAMBIA

ZIMBABWE

ANGOLA

BOTSWANA

SWAZILAND

NAMIBIA

LESOTHO

SOUTH
AFRICA

CONGO

GABON

SAO TOME & PRINCIPE

ATLANTIC OCEAN

AFRICA

Both tropics and the equator
run through Africa, the
warmest of all the continents.
The land around the tropics is
starved of rain, creating great
deserts such as the Sahara and
the Kalahari. In contrast,
high rainfall around the
equator has produced lush
tropical rainforests.

NORTHWEST AFRICA

SPANNING THE continent of Africa from the Atlantic to the Red Sea, the Sahara is the world's largest desert, covering 3.5 million sq miles (9 million sq km). Drought and the overuse of land for farming are causing the Sahara to spread into the Sahel (semiarid grasslands). Italy, the U.K., Spain, and France have had colonies in this region.

Strait of Gibraltar
Ceuta *(to Spain)* Melil *(to Spa*
Tangier
Casablanca RABAT
M O R O C C O Fez
Marrakesh
Agadir *L A S M T*
A T L A S Béc

ATLANTIC OCEAN
EL AAIUN
Dakhla
WESTERN SAHARA
M A U R I T A N I A
M

Morocco occupied the whole of Western Sahara in 1979.

INDUSTRY
Oil, gas, phosphates, tourism, olives, dates, fruit. Morocco and Tunisia attract millions of tourists every year and are also leading phosphate producers. Algeria and Libya have significant oil reserves.

MOROCCO
P 27 million
L Arabic

CLIMATE
Coastal areas have a temperate climate with hot, dry summers and wet winters. Mountain areas are cooler. Most areas are affected by the many different kinds of Sahara wind, such as the *sirocco*, the *chergui*, and the *chili*.

NATURAL FEATURES
The Atlas Mountains exten over 1,500 miles (2,410 km) from the Canary Islands in the Atlantic to Tunisia. Like the Alps, the Atla Mountains were formed when the continental plates of Europe and Africa pushed together.

A   B   C   D

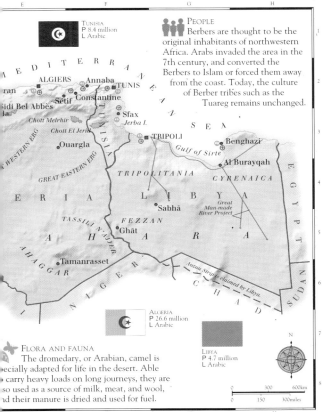

TUNISIA
P 8.4 million
L Arabic

PEOPLE
Berbers are thought to be the original inhabitants of northwestern Africa. Arabs invaded the area in the 7th century, and converted the Berbers to Islam or forced them away from the coast. Today, the culture of Berber tribes such as the Tuareg remains unchanged.

MEDITERRANEAN

ALGIERS Annaba
ran TUNIS
idi Bel Abbès Sétif Constantine
la.
Chott Melrhir Sfax
Chott El Jerid Jerba I.

SEA

TRIPOLI Benghazi

Ouargla Gulf of Sirte Al Burayqah

GREAT EASTERN ERG

TRIPOLITANIA CYRENAICA

ERIA LIBYA

Sabhā Great Man-made River Project

TASSILI N'AJJER FEZZAN

A Ghāt

HAGGAR AHAGGAR

Tamanrasset

NIGER

CHAD

Aozou Strip is claimed by Libya

EGYPT

SUDAN

ALGERIA
P 26.6 million
L Arabic

FLORA AND FAUNA
The dromedary, or Arabian, camel is ecially adapted for life in the desert. Able carry heavy loads on long journeys, they are so used as a source of milk, meat, and wool, nd their manure is dried and used for fuel.

LIBYA
P 4.7 million
L Arabic

N

0   300   600km
0   150   300miles

NORTHEAST AFRICA

THE NILE, THE LONGEST river in the world, carries rich mud from the highlands of Sudan into Egypt, creating some of the most fertile land in the world. About 99 percent of Egypt's population live on the river's banks. Ethiopia, Somalia, and Sudan have been beset by drought, famine, and war, so about half of Africa's 4.5 million refugees come from this area.

EGYPT
P 54.8 million
L Arabic

HISTORY

Hieroglyphics were a set of mysterious symbols until the discovery of the Rosetta Stone in 1799. The Stone is inscribed in three different scripts: ancient Greek, demotic, and hieroglyphs. By comparing the royal names in the scripts, hieroglyphs were finally deciphered 25 years later.

ERITREA
P 3.5 million
L Tigrinya, Arabic

MEDITERRANEAN SEA

Alexandria
El Mansûra
Port Saïd
Ismâ'ilîya
Suez
SINAI
Gulf of Aqaba
Gulf of Suez
CAIRO
Giza · Helwân
El Faiyûm
El Minya
Asyût
Sohâg
Valley of the Kings
Luxor
Qena
Aswân · Philae
L. Nasser
Abu Simbel

RED SEA

ISRAEL

NUBIAN

E G Y P T

LIBYA

LIBYAN DESERT

Nile

Qattâra Depression

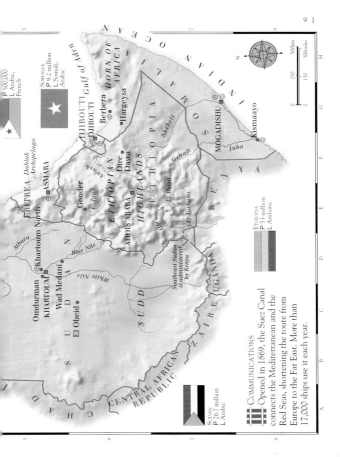

P 500,000
L Arabic,
French

SOMALIA
P 9.2 million
L Somali,
Arabic

HORN OF AFRICA

INDIAN OCEAN

GULF OF ADEN

DJIBOUTI
● DJIBOUTI

● Berbera

● Hargeysa

ERITREA *Dahlak Archipelago*

● ASMARA

MOGADISHU

Shebeli

● Dire
● Dawa
Mek'elē

● Gonder

L. Tana

ETHIOPIAN

Genale

Juba

● Kismaayo

S O M A L I A

K E N Y A

ADDIS ABABA ●

HIGHLANDS

EAST HIGHLANDS

Omo

L. Abaya

L. Turkana

Southeast Sudan
is administered
by Kenya

ETHIOPIA
P 53 million
L Amharic

Atbara

Khartoum North

● Omdurman
◎ KHARTOUM

S U D A N

Blue Nile

● Wad Medani

UGANDA

ZAIRE

● El Obeid

White Nile

S U D D

CENTRAL AFRICAN
REPUBLIC

C H A D

SUDAN
P 26.7 million
L Arabic

COMMUNICATIONS

Opened in 1869, the Suez Canal
connects the Mediterranean and the
Red Seas, shortening the route from
Europe to the Far East. More than
17,000 ships use it each year.

N

0   250   500km
0   150   300miles

WEST AFRICA

BY 1914, MANY European
countries, such as France,
Britain, and Portugal, had
divided up almost all of
Africa between them.
Despite independence,
foreign companies still
own many of the
coffee and cocoa
plantations in the region.

GAMBIA
P 920,000
L English

■ INDUSTRY
Bauxite, oil, gypsum, cocoa,
phosphates, peanuts, fishing.
This region produces nearly half
of the world's supply of cocoa
beans. The world's largest deposits
of gypsum are found in Mauritania.

☁ CLIMATE
Coastal areas have
a tropical climate, with
high temperatures and
one or two rainy seasons.
The hot and dry Sahel
is marked by the dusty
harmattan wind.

GUINEA
P 7.7 million
L French

GUINEA-BISSAU
P 1 million
L Portuguese

SIERRA LEONE
P 4.4 million
L English

WESTERN SAHARA

C. Blanc
C. Timiris

S   A
MAURITANIA
⊕⊕ NOUAKCHOTT
L. Rkiz
Senegal
SENEGAL   S
DAKAR ■⊕
BANJUL ■ GAMBIA   BAMAKO ■
BISSAU ⊕
GUINEA-BISSAU   G   U   I   N
Bijagós
Archipelago   Niger
CONAKRY ⊕
⊕⊕ FREETOWN ■ SIERRA
LEONE   de Kossi
MONROVIA ⊕ ⊕ YAMOUSSOUK
LIBERIA
Ivo

ATLANTIC OCEAN

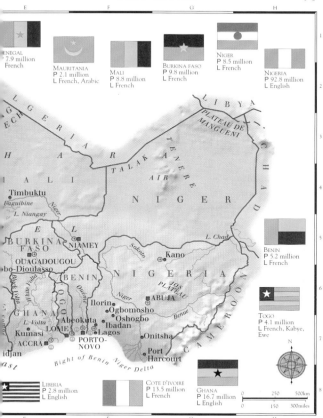

SENEGAL
P 7.9 million
L French

MAURITANIA
P 2.1 million
L French, Arabic

MALI
P 8.8 million
L French

BURKINA FASO
P 9.8 million
L French

NIGER
P 8.5 million
L French

NIGERIA
P 92.8 million
L English

BENIN
P 5.2 million
L French

TOGO
P 4.1 million
L French, Kabye,
Ewe

LIBERIA
P 2.8 million
L English

COTE D'IVOIRE
P 13.5 million
L French

GHANA
P 16.7 million
L English

CENTRAL AFRICA

MUCH OF THIS region is covered in dense tropical rainforest, drained by the Congo (Zaire) River, which flows in a huge arc on its way to the Atlantic. In the 16th century Portugal and Spain set up trading posts on the west coast as part of the slave trade. Millions of Africans from this region were sent as slaves to the New World. Many people in coastal areas still speak Spanish and Portuguese.

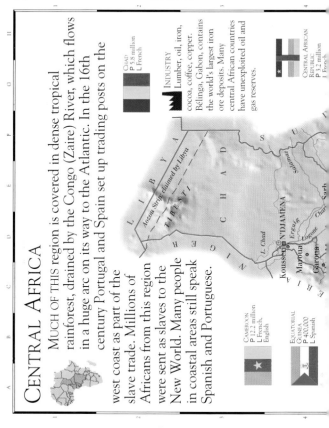

CHAD
P 5.8 million
L French

INDUSTRY
Lumber, oil, iron, cocoa, coffee, copper. Bélinga, Gabon, contains the world's largest iron ore deposits. Many central African countries have unexploited oil and gas reserves.

CENTRAL AFRICAN REPUBLIC
P 3.2 million
L French

CAMEROON
P 12.2 million
L French, English

EQUATORIAL GUINEA
P 400,000
L Spanish

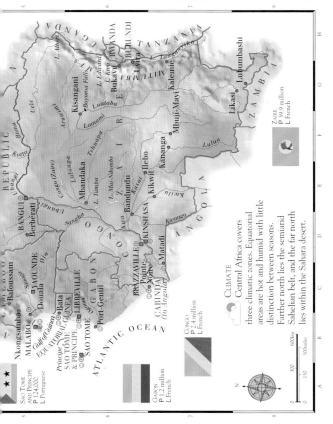

SAO TOME
AND PRINCIPE
P 124,000
L Portuguese

GABON
P 1.2 million
L French

CONGO
P 2.4 million
L French

ZAIRE
P 39.9 million
L French

CLIMATE
Central Africa covers three climatic zones. Equatorial areas are hot and humid with little distinction between seasons. Farther north lies the semiarid Sahelian belt, and the far north lies within the Sahara desert.

Nkongsamba
MALABO
EQUATORIAL GUINEA
Gulf of Guinea
Bata
Principe
SAO TOME & PRINCIPE
SAO TOME
Port-Genti
LIBREVILLE
GABON
BRAZZAVILLE
Pointe-Noire
CABINDA
(to Angola)
Matadi
KINSHASA

Baloussam
YAOUNDE
Douala
Dja
Sanaga
Ogoou
CONGO
Kwango
Kwa
Kasai
Kwilu
ANGOLA

REPUBLIC
BANGUI
Berbérati
Ubangi
Sangha
Kotto
Bomu
Uele
Ubangi (Zaire)
Lulonga
Tshuapa
Lomela
Lake Mai-Ndombe
Bandundu
Kikwit
Kwilu
Kamanga
Lulua
Ilebo
Kasai

Uele
Araouimi
Lomami
Bomu
Kisangani
Boyoma Falls
Lualaba
Z A I R E
Tshuapa
Sankuru
Mbandaka
L. Tumba
Kananga
Mbuji-Mayi

UGANDA
L. Albert
RWANDA
BURUNDI
TANZANIA
L. Edward
L. Kivu
Bukavu
L. Tanganyika
MITUMBA
Kalemie
Likasi
Lubumbashi
ZAMBIA
Kuba

ATLANTIC OCEAN

N

0   100   300km
0   150   300miles

CENTRAL EAST AFRICA

LARGE AREAS OF savanna, or grassland, in central Africa provide grazing for domestic and wild animals alike. Industry is poorly developed in the region – Zambia, Rwanda, Burundi, and Uganda suffer from having no seaports. Lake Victoria is the largest lake in Africa, and a source of the Nile River.

FLORA AND FAUNA

Poaching remains a major problem in this area. To combat this, all the countries in this region have set up wildlife parks to protect animals such as elephants and zebra.

INDUSTRY

Tobacco, coffee, tea, tourism, cloves, copper. Zambia is the world's fifth-largest producer of copper. Wildlife parks in this region

KENYA
P 25.2 million
L Swahili

UGANDA
P 18.7 million
L English

RWANDA
P 7.5 million
L French,
Kinyarwanda

R

SOMALIA

ETHIOPIA

SUDAN

CHALBI
DESERT

KENYA

NAIROBI

Tana

Galana

L. Turkana

Southeast Sudan
is administered
by Kenya

GREAT RIFT VALLEY

ABERDARE RANGE

L. Kyoga

UGANDA

KAMPALA

Albert Nile

Victoria
Nile

L. Albert

L. Eduard

L. Edward

KIGALI

RWANDA

BURUNDI

BUJUMBURA

Lake
Victoria

Mwanza

Mara

L. Eyasi

ZAÏRE

OCEAN

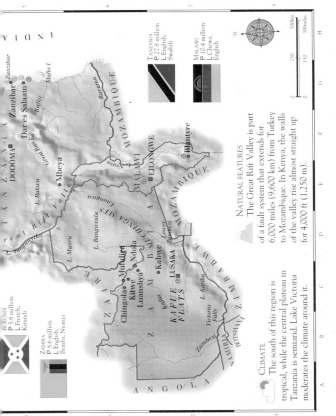

INDIAN

Zanzibar • Zanzibar

Mafia I.

DODOMA
Dar es Salaam

TANZANIA
P 27.8 million
L English,
Swahili

MALAWI
P 10.4 million
L Chewa,
English

Rufiji

Ruvuma

MOZAMBIQUE

L. Rukwa

Great Ruaha

Mbeya

L. Nyasa

BLANTYRE

LILONGWE

MALAWI

Great Rift Valley

L. Tanganyika

L. Mweru

L. Bangweulu

MUCHINGA MTS.

Luangwa

MOZAMBIQUE

Mulilima

Ndola

Chingola
Kitwe
Luanshya

Kabwe

LUSAKA

Lower Zambezi

L. Kariba

KAFUE FLATS

Kafue

Victoria
Falls

ZAMBIA

ZIMBABWE

Zambezi

BOTSWANA

NAMIBIA

ANGOLA

BURUNDI
P 5.8 million
L French,
Kirundi

ZAMBIA
P 8.6 million
L English,
Bemba, Nyanja

NATURAL FEATURES

The Great Rift Valley is part
of a fault system that extends for
6,000 miles (9,600 km) from Turkey
to Mozambique. In Kenya, the walls
of the valley rise almost straight up
for 4,000 ft (1,250 m).

CLIMATE

The south of this region is
tropical, while the central plateau in
Tanzania is semiarid. Lake Victoria
moderates the climate around it.

N

500 km
250
300 miles
150
0
0

SOUTHERN AFRICA

THE RICHEST DEPOSITS of valuable minerals in Africa, such as gold and diamonds, are found in its southern region. Many countries surrounding South Africa rely on it for work and trade. Racial segregation under apartheid operated from 1948 until South Africa's first multiracial elections were held in 1994. Namibia won its independence from South Africa in 1990, but neighboring Angola has been in a state of civil war since 1975.

MOZAMBIQUE
P 16.1 million
L Portuguese

ZIMBABWE
P 10.6 million
L English

BOTSWANA
P 1.3 million
L English

ANGOLA
P 9.9 million
L Portuguese

TANZANIA

L. Nyasa

Ruvuma

Nacala

Lurio

MALAWI

ZAMBIA

CONGO

ZAIRE

CABINDA
(to Angola)

Cabinda

LUANDA

Capenda
Camulemba

ANGOLA

Cuito

Cuango

Lobito

Huambo

ATLANTIC

Mozambique Channel

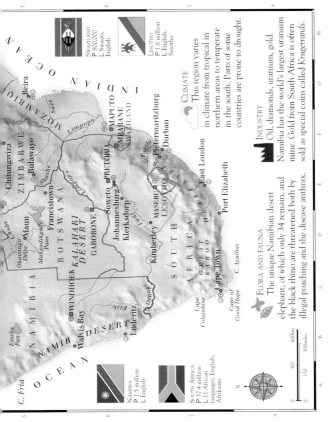

SWAZILAND
P 800,000
L Swisati,
English

LESOTHO
P 1.8 million
L English,
Sesotho

CLIMATE

This region varies in climate from tropical in northern areas to temperate in the south. Parts of some countries are prone to drought.

INDUSTRY

Oil, diamonds, uranium, gold. Namibia has the world's largest uranium mine. Gold from South Africa is often sold as special coins called *Krugerrands*.

FLORA AND FAUNA

The unique Namibian desert elephant, of which only 34 remain, and the black rhino are threatened both by illegal poaching and the disease anthrax.

NAMIBIA
P 1.5 million
L English

SOUTH AFRICA
P 37.4 million
L 11 African
languages, English,
Afrikaans

INDIAN OCEAN

Beira

MOZAMBIQUE

Save

Limpopo

MAPUTO

MBABANE
SWAZILAND

Chitungwiza

ZIMBABWE

Bulawayo

Francistown

Shashe

Limpopo

PRETORIA

Soweto

Johannesburg

Klerksdorp

Kimberley

Tugela

Pietermaritzburg

Durban

East London

MASERU
LESOTHO

Orange

GREAT KAROO

Port Elizabeth

SOUTH AFRICA

TRANSVAAL

Cape Town

C. Agulhas

Cape of
Good Hope

Cape
Columbine

Okavango
Delta

Chobe

Maun

Makgadikgadi
Pans

KALAHARI
DESERT

BOTSWANA

GABORONE

C. Fria

Etosha
Pan

NAMIBIA

WINDHOEK

Walvis Bay

NAMIB DESERT

Lüderitz

Fish

Orange

ATLANTIC OCEAN

N

0   150   300
0   300   600km
300miles

INDIAN OCEAN

THE SMALLEST OF the world's oceans, the Indian Ocean has some 5,000 islands scattered across its area. Beneath its surface, three great mountain ranges converge toward the ocean's center – an area of strong seismic and volcanic activity. The ocean's greatest depth, 24,400 ft (7,440 m), is in the Java Trench.

FLORA AND FAUNA
Owing to Madagascar's position off the African coast, many of its animals, such as tenrecs, lemurs, and fossas, are unique.

ENVIRONMENT
The Indian Ocean is at risk of pollution from tankers carrying oil from the Persian Gulf, which is already badly polluted.

CLIMATE
The monsoon winds blow over the Indian Ocean – from the southwest or from the northeast according to the season. The southwesterly monsoon brings heavy rains to southern Asia.

COMOROS
P 497,000
L Arabic,
French

MALDIVES
P 240,000
L Dhvehi

SEYCHELLES
P 68,000

Port Said
Suez
Suez Canal
Kuwait City
Persian Gulf
Aden
Gulf of Aden
Djibouti
RED SEA
A R A B I A
Ras
al Hadd
ARABIAN SEA
Karachi
Bombay
Madras
Cochin
Sri Lanka
MALDIVES
Laccadive Is.
(to India)
Socotra
(to Yemen)
L. Minicoy
Nicobar Is.
Andaman Is.
(to India)
ANDAMAN SEA
Bay of Bengal
Calcutta
Indus
Ganges
Irrawaddy
Mekong
Rangoon
Gulf of Thailand
SOUTH

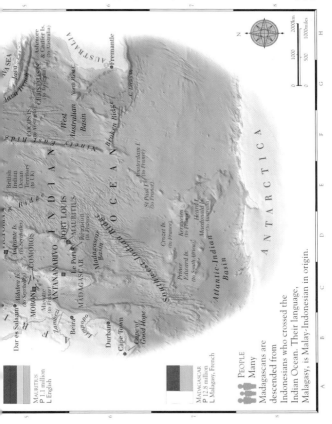

JAVA SEA
Java
Java Trench
CHRISTMAS I.
(to Australia)
COCOS IS.
(to Australia)
Ashmore
& Cartier Is.
(to Australia)
AUSTRALIA
○ Fremantle
North West C.
C. Leeuwin

West
Australian
Basin
Broken Ridge

INDIAN
OCEAN
British
Indian
Ocean
Territory
(to UK)
East Indian Ridge
Cuvier
Plateau
Amsterdam I.
(to France)
St Paul I.
(to France)

ANTARCTICA

Aldabra Is.
(to Seychelles)
Amirante Is.
(to Seychelles)
Dar es Salaam ●
MORONI ■
Mayotte
(to France)
Jambica
COMOROS
ANTANANARIVO ■
PORT LOUIS
Le Port ●
Réunion
(to France)
MAURITIUS
Madagascar
Basin
Crozet Is.
(to France)
Prince
Edward Is.
(to South Africa)
Kerguelen
(to France)
Heard I.
(to Australia)
McDonald Is.
(to Australia)

Beira ●
Bazaruto
MADAGASCAR
South West Indian Ridge
Atlantic-Indian
Basin

Durban ●
Cape Town ●
Cape of
Good Hope

PEOPLE
Many
Madagascans are
descended from
Indonesians who crossed the
Indian Ocean. Their language,
Malagasy, is Malay-Indonesian in origin.

N

0   1000   2000km
0   500   1000miles

A   B   C   D   E   F   G   H

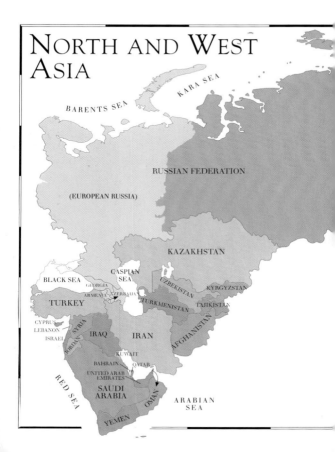

NORTH AND WEST ASIA

BARENTS SEA

KARA SEA

RUSSIAN FEDERATION

(EUROPEAN RUSSIA)

KAZAKHSTAN

CASPIAN SEA

BLACK SEA

GEORGIA

ARMENIA AZERBAIJAN

UZBEKISTAN

KYRGYZSTAN

TURKEY

TURKMENISTAN

TAJIKISTAN

CYPRUS

LEBANON

ISRAEL

JORDAN

SYRIA

IRAQ

IRAN

AFGHANISTAN

KUWAIT

BAHRAIN

QATAR

UNITED ARAB EMIRATES

RED SEA

SAUDI ARABIA

OMAN

ARABIAN SEA

YEMEN

NORTH AND WEST ASIA

Asia is the largest continent in the world, occupying nearly one-third of the world's total land area. In the south, the Arabian Peninsula is mostly hot, dry desert. In the north lie cold deserts, treeless plains called steppes and the largest needleleaf forest in the world, which stretches from Siberia to northern Europe.

TURKEY

BRIDGING THE CONTINENTS of Europe and Asia, Turkey was once the center of the Ottoman Empire, which at one time controlled one-quarter of Europe. Independent of the U.K. in 1960, Cyprus was invaded by Turkey in 1974. Southern Cyprus is Greek; Turkish Northern Cyprus is recognized only by Turkey.

TURKEY
P 59.9 million
L Turkish

INDUSTRY
Wheat, corn, sugar beets, nuts, fruit, cotton, tobacco, tourism. Carpet-weaving is a tradition dating back centuries. Figs and peaches are grown on the coast of the Mediterranean.

ENVIRONMENT
Turkey's dam-building projects on the Tigris and Euphrates Rivers have met with disapproval from Syria and Iraq, whose own rivers will have reduced flow as a result.

PEOPLE
The Kurds are Turkey's main minority group and one of the largest groups of stateless people in the world. Their homeland, Kurdistan, straddles three countries: Turkey, Iraq, and Iran. Kurds are fighting for recognition of their rights within Turkey.

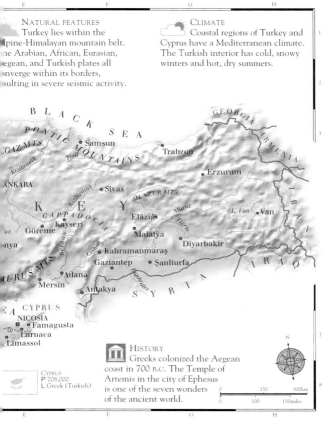

NATURAL FEATURES

Turkey lies within the Alpine-Himalayan mountain belt. The Arabian, African, Eurasian, Aegean, and Turkish plates all converge within its borders, resulting in severe seismic activity.

CLIMATE

Coastal regions of Turkey and Cyprus have a Mediterranean climate. The Turkish interior has cold, snowy winters and hot, dry summers.

BLACK SEA

GEORGIA

ARMENIA

PONTIC MOUNTAINS

GAZ MTS.

Kızılırmak

Yeşil

• Samsun

• Trabzon

ANKARA

Kızılırmak

• Sivas

• Erzurum

IRAN

MUNZUR MTS.

K E Y

CAPPADOCIA

• Kayseri

Elazığ

Mucat

L. Van

• Van

-uz

• Göreme

Seyhan

Malatya

Tigris

-nya

Ceyhan

• Kahramanmaraş

• Diyarbakir

TAURUS MTS.

• Gaziantep

• Şanlıurfa

IRAQ

• Adana

Euphrates

• Mersin

• Antakya

SYRIA

EA

CYPRUS

NICOSIA

• Famagusta

• Larnaca

• Limassol

CYPRUS
P 708,000
L Greek (Turkish)

HISTORY

Greeks colonized the Aegean coast in 700 B.C. The Temple of Artemis in the city of Ephesus is one of the seven wonders of the ancient world.

N

0   150   300km
0   100   150miles

THE NEAR EAST

AT THE JUNCTION of Africa, Asia, and Europe, the Near East is a mosaic of deserts, mountains, and fertile valleys. After centuries of conflict, there are now hopes for peace in the region. Lebanon is beginning to emerge from a civil war that began in 1975 and the disputes over territories in Israel, such as the West Bank and the Gaza Strip, are starting to be resolved.

LEBANON
P 2.8 million
L Arabic

INDUSTRY
Oil, potash, cotton, fruit. Water is in short supply in this region and special irrigation techniques are used in order to avoid waste. Syria's main cash crop is cotton.

ISRAEL
P 5.3 million
L Hebrew, Arabic

Map labels

Türkiye

At Ḥasakah

AL JAZIRAH

Euphrates

T U R K E Y

L. Assad

Ḥalab

Oronts

Al

Lādhiqīyah

Ḥamāh

Ḥimṣ

Tripoli

Beirut

MEDITERRANEAN SEA

LEBANON

SHAMIYAH DESERT

S Y R I A

DAMASCUS

I R A Q

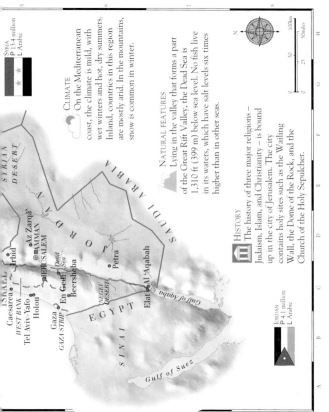

SYRIA
P 13.4 million
L Arabic

CLIMATE
On the Mediterranean coast, the climate is mild, with wet winters and hot, dry summers. Inland, countries in this region are mostly arid. In the mountains, snow is common in winter.

NATURAL FEATURES
Lying in the valley that forms a part of the Great Rift Valley, the Dead Sea is 1,310 ft (399 m) below sea level. No fish live in its waters, which have salt levels six times higher than in other seas.

HISTORY
The history of three major religions – Judaism, Islam, and Christianity – is bound up in the city of Jerusalem. The city contains holy sites such as the Wailing Wall, the Dome of the Rock, and the Church of the Holy Sepulcher.

JORDAN
P 4.1 million
L Arabic

N

0   50   100km
0   25   50miles

ISRAEL
Caesarea
Tel Aviv-Yafo
Holon
WEST BANK
Irbid
Az Zarqā'
AMMAN
JERUSALEM
Dead Sea
En Gedi
Beersheba
Gaza
GAZA STRIP
NEGEV DESERT
Petra
Elat Al 'Aqabah
Gulf of Aqaba
EGYPT
SINAI
Gulf of Suez

SYRIAN DESERT
JORDAN
SAUDI ARABIA

THE MIDDLE EAST

ISLAM WAS FOUNDED in A.D. 570 in Mecca, Saudi Arabia, and spread throughout the Middle East, where today it is the main religion. Oil has brought wealth to the region, but in 1991 the area was financially devastated by the Gulf War.

INDUSTRY
Oil, natural gas, fishing, carpet-weaving, offshore banking. Saudi Arabia has the world's largest oil reserves. Over 60 percent of the world's desalination plants are used in this region to make seawater drinkable.

CLIMATE
Most of the countries in this region are semiarid, with low rainfall. Inland, summer temperatures can reach 119°F (48°C) with winter temperatures falling to freezing.

HISTORY
Ancient civilizations developed about 5,500 years ago in Mesopotamia, between the Tigris and Euphrates Rivers. The Sumerian civilization had advanced methods of irrigation, sophisticated architecture, and a complex form of writing called cuneiform.

IRAQ
P 20.7 mill
L Arabic

SAUDI ARABIA
P 17.5 million
L Arabic

KUWAIT
P 2.1 million
L Arabic

BAHRAIN
P 570,000
L Arabic

QATAR
P 500,000
L Arabic

UNITED ARAB EMIRATES
P 2.6 million
L Arabic

YEMEN
P 12.5 million
L Arabic

EGYPT · JORD

Gulf of Aqaba

HEJAZ

RED

SEA

Mecca

Jedda

Hodei
Al Muk
Bab el Ma

IRAN
P 61.6 million
L Farsi

OMAN
P 1.6 million
L Arabic

E   G   H

TURKEY
AZERBAIJAN

L. Urmia
Ardabīl
CASPIAN SEA
TURKMENISTAN

Mosul
Irbil
Zanjān
Rasht
SYRIA
Kirkūk
Sanandaj
As Sulaymānīyah
Sarī
Mashhad

I R A Q
TEHRAN
Bakhtarān Qom
Semnān
ELBURZ MTS

BAGHDAD
Īlām
Arāk
DASHT-E KAVIR

Karbalā Al-Hillah
Dezfūl
Eṣfahān

An-Najaf
Al Amārah
Euphrates

An Nāṣirīyah
Aḥvāz
Yazd
DASHT-E LUT

Al-Basrah
Ābādān
B A K H T I A R I

Buraydah
KUWAIT CITY
Yāsūj
KUWAIT Shīrāz
Kermān
Zāhedān

NEJD
Ad
Dammām
Bandar-e Abbās
Jaz Mūrian
Salt Lake

RIYADH
AD DAHNA
MANAMA BAHRAIN
DOHA
Al Hufūf QATAR
Strait of
Hormuz
Khasab
(to Oman)

S A U D I
ARABIA
ABU DHABI Dubai
UNITED ARAB
EMIRATES
Gulf of Oman

MUSCAT

RUB' AL KHALI
O M A N

Masirah I.
Gulf of Masīrah

RAMLAT AS SAB'ATAYN
'A
Y E M E N
HADHRAMAUT
ARABIAN SEA

en

Persian
Gulf

0   300   600km
0   150   300miles

E   F   G   H

1
2
3
4
5
6
7
8

CENTRAL ASIA

FOR CENTURIES, many people in central Asia lived in mountains as nomads, or in cities that sprang up along the Silk Road. When the region came under Soviet rule, industry was developed and irrigation schemes made farming possible.

INDUSTRY
Cotton, gold, gas, sulfur, mercury, opium, hydroelectricity. Uzbekistan has the largest single gold mine in the world. Tajikistan has 14 percent of the world's known uranium resources.

HISTORY
In the early 1900s, most of this region, except for Afghanistan, came under Soviet rule, which restricted the use of local languages and Islam. Today, these newly independent countries are resuming the religions, languages, and traditions of their past.

TURKMENISTAN
P 3.9 million
L Turkmen, Russian

ENVIRONMENT
Crop irrigation draws water from the Amu Darya River, reducing the amount of water flowing into the Aral Sea. By the year 2000 the Sea will have shrunk to a third of its original size.

USTYURT PLATEAU

ARAL SEA

TURAN LOWLAND

L. Sarykamysh

Nukus

UZ

Zaliv Kara-Bogaz-Gol

Tashauz

Urgench

CASPIAN SEA

Krasnovodsk

Nebit Dag

TURKMENISTAN

ASHKABAD

I

N

He

A F

Kara

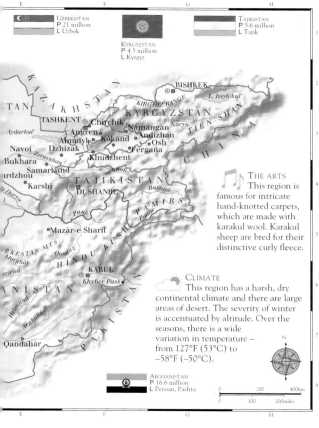

UZBEKISTAN
P 21 million
L Uzbek

KYRGYZSTAN
P 4.5 million
L Kyrgyz

TAJIKISTAN
P 5.6 million
L Tajik

KAZAKHSTAN

KYRGYZSTAN
BISHKEK
KIRGHIZ RANGE   L. Issyk-kul'
TIEN SHAN

TASHKENT   Chirchik
Angren   Namangan   *Naryn*   Andizhan
Almalyk   Kokand   Osh
Aydarkul'   Dzhizak   Fergana
Navoi   *Zeravshan*   Khudzhent   CHINA
Bukhara   Samarkand
Chardzhou   Karshi   TAJIKISTAN
    DUSHANBE   *Surkhob*   PAMIRS
    Pyanj   *Bartang*
Amu Darya   *Panai*
Mazār-e Sharif
TURKESTAN MTS.   *Qunduz*
Morghāb   HINDU KUSH   PAKISTAN
Harirud   KABUL
AFGHANISTAN   Khyber Pass
Helmand
Arghandāb
Qandahār

THE ARTS
This region is famous for intricate hand-knotted carpets, which are made with karakul wool. Karakul sheep are bred for their distinctive curly fleece.

CLIMATE
This region has a harsh, dry continental climate and there are large areas of desert. The severity of winter is accentuated by altitude. Over the seasons, there is a wide variation in temperature – from 127°F (53°C) to –58°F (–50°C).

AFGHANISTAN
P 16.6 million
L Persian, Pashtu

N

0   200   400km
0   100   200miles

THE RUSSIAN FEDERATION AND KAZAKHSTAN

THE URAL mountains separate European and Asian Russia, which extends from the frozen arctic lands in the north to the central Asian deserts in the south. In 1991, Kazakhstan became the last Soviet republic to gain independence.

CLIMATE
Kazakhstan has a continental climate. Winter temperatures in Russia vary little from north to south, but fall sharply in the east, especially in Siberia.

PEOPLE
There are 57 nationalities, each with their own territories, within the Russian Federation. A further 95 groups are without territories of their own, although these groups make up only six percent of the total population.

FINLAND
ESTONIA
LATVIA
BELARUS
UKRAINE
GEORGIA
UZBEKISTAN
TURKMENISTAN
UZBEKISTAN

Murmansk
BARENTS S
St. Petersburg
Pskov
Novgorod
Arkhangel'sk
Smolensk
MOSCOW
Yaroslavl'
Tula
Ryazan'
Kirov
Voronezh
Penza
Kazan'
Izhevsk
Perm'
Rostov-na-Donu
Simbirsk
Naberezhnyye Che
Saratov
Samara
Yekaterinbu
Krasnodar
Tol'yatti
Ufa
Chelyabin
Volgograd
Ural'sk
Orenburg
O
Astrakhan'
Ural
Kustanai
Grozny
Atyrau
Aktyubinsk
Ishi
CASPIAN SEA
Emba
Tselinograd
KIRGHIZ STEPPE
L. Tengiz
ARAL
Karaganda
SEA
KAZAKHSTAN
Kzyl-Orda
L. Balk
Syr Darya
Chu
Shimkent
ALMA-A

URAL MOUNTAINS

KAZAKHSTAN
P 17 million
L Kazakh

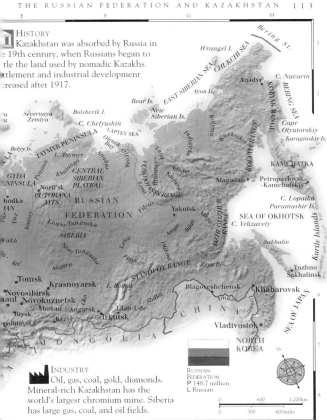

HISTORY

Kazakhstan was absorbed by Russia in the 19th century, when Russians began to settle the land used by nomadic Kazakhs. Settlement and industrial development increased after 1917.

INDUSTRY

Oil, gas, coal, gold, diamonds. Mineral-rich Kazakhstan has the world's largest chromium mine. Siberia has large gas, coal, and oil fields.

RUSSIAN
FEDERATION
P 148.7 million
L Russian

Bering St.

Wrangel I.

EAST SIBERIAN SEA

CHUKCHI SEA

Anadyr'

C. Navarin

Ayon Is.

BERING SEA

Bear Is.

New Siberian Is.

KORYAK RANGE

Cape Olyutorskiy

Karaginskiy Is.

Bolshevik I.

Severnaya Zemlya

C. Chelyuskin

LAPTEV SEA

Olenёk Bay

TAYMYR PENINSULA

L. Taymyr

Khatanga

Kotuy

Kolyma

KOLYMA RANGE

KAMCHATKA

Magadan

Petropavlovsk-Kamchatskiy

Belyy Is.

GYDA PENINSULA

CENTRAL SIBERIAN PLATEAU

Pyasina

Kureyka

Vilyuy

Anabar

Olenёk

Lena

Indigirka

Yana

Alazeya

Indigirka

Omolon

C. Lopatka

Paramushir Is.

Noril'sk

PUTORANA MTS.

RUSSIAN

FEDERATION

SIBERIA

Yenisey

Lower Tunguska

Stony Tunguska

Angara

Lena

Vilyuy

VERKHOYANSK RANGE

Aldan

Maya

Yakutsk

DZHUGDZHUR RANGE

C. Yelizavety

SEA OF OKHOTSK

Sakhalin

Tomsk

Krasnoyarsk

L. Baikal

Shilka

STANOVOY RANGE

Zeya Res.

Kurile Islands

Novosibirsk

Barnaul

Novokuznetsk

Abakan

Angarsk

Ulan-Ude

Irkutsk

Blagoveshchensk

Amur

Khabarovsk

SEA OF JAPAN

Biysk

Kyzyl

CHINA

Vladivostok

MONGOLIA

NORTH KOREA

Yuzhno-Sakhalinsk

0   600   1,200km
0   300   600miles

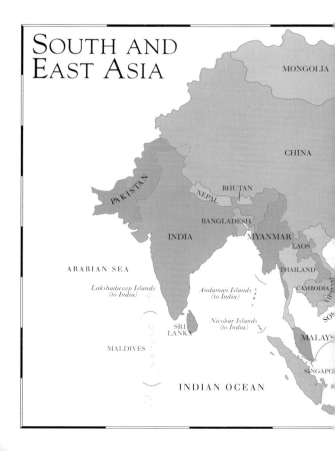

SOUTH AND EAST ASIA

MONGOLIA

CHINA

PAKISTAN

NEPAL

BHUTAN

BANGLADESH

INDIA

MYANMAR

LAOS

THAILAND

CAMBODIA

ARABIAN SEA

Lakshadweep Islands
(to India)

Andaman Islands
(to India)

Nicobar Islands
(to India)

SRI
LANKA

MALDIVES

MALAYS

SINGAPO

SO

INDIAN OCEAN

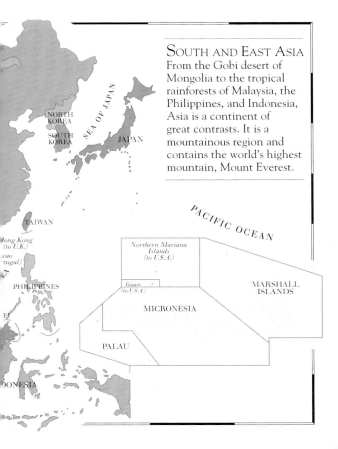

SOUTH AND EAST ASIA

From the Gobi desert of Mongolia to the tropical rainforests of Malaysia, the Philippines, and Indonesia, Asia is a continent of great contrasts. It is a mountainous region and contains the world's highest mountain, Mount Everest.

NORTH KOREA

SOUTH KOREA

SEA OF JAPAN

JAPAN

TAIWAN

Hong Kong
(to U.K.)

cao
rtugal)

PHILIPPINES

PACIFIC OCEAN

Northern Mariana
Islands
(to U.S.A.)

Guam
(to U.S.A.)

MARSHALL
ISLANDS

MICRONESIA

PALAU

ONESIA

THE INDIAN SUBCONTINENT

SEPARATED FROM THE rest of Asia by the Himalayas, India is the second most populated country after China. It is estimated that India's population will overtake that of China by 2030. To the north, Nepal and Bhutan lie nestled in the Himalayas between China and India, and to the south lies Sri Lanka, once known as Ceylon.

INDUSTRY
Tea, jute, iron, cut diamonds, cotton, rice, sugarcane, textiles. Bangladesh exports 80 percent of the world's jute fiber. Sri Lanka is the largest tea exporter in the world. Pakistan is a major exporter of rice.

HISTORY
In 1947, when India gained independence, religious differences led to the creation of two countries – Hindu India and Muslim Pakistan. In 1971, a short civil war broke out between East and West Pakistan and East Pakistan became Bangladesh.

INDIA
P 879.5 million
L Hindi, English

NATURAL FEATURES
The Himalayas were formed as a result of a violent crumpling of the Earth's crust. Frequent earthquakes indicate that the process is continuing. The highest peaks in the world, including Mount Everest, are in this mountain system.

AFGHANISTAN
IRAN
CHAGAI HILLS
TOBA-KAKAR RANGE
PAKISTAN
MAKRAN
Indus
Karachi
Hyderaba
Gulf of Kutch
Rajk
ARABIAN SEA
Gul
Khan

0   350   70
0   200   400m

PAKISTAN
P 122.4 million
L Urdu

BHUTAN
P 1.6 million
L Dzongkha

NEPAL
P 20.4 million
L Nepali

BANGLADESH
P 119.3 million
L Bengali

SRI LANKA
P 17.7 million
L Sinhalese,
Tamil

CLIMATE
Sri Lanka and southern India are tropical, with little seasonal variation in temperature. The north has a cold alpine climate. Cyclones regularly build up in the Bay of Bengal. Bangladesh is often flooded during the monsoon.

Peshawar
ISLAMABAD
Rawalpindi Srinagar
Gujranwala
Lahore Amritsar
Jalandhar
Faisalabad Ludhiana Chandigarh
Multan

NEW DELHI Meerut
Jaipur Agra
Bareilly KATHMANDU
Lucknow THIMPHU
Gwalior BHUTAN
Kota Kanpur Varanasi Patna Brahmaputra
Jodhpur Allahabad Guwahati
Ahmadabad Bhopal Jabalpur Dhanbad DACCA Imphal
INDIA Rajshahi BANGLADESH Agartala
Vadodara Indore Narmada Ranchi Calcutta Khulna
Surat Tapti Nagpur Chittagong
Nasik Mahanadi
Thane DECCAN Godavari
Bombay Pune Sholapur
Hyderabad EASTERN GHATS Vishakhapatnam
Panaji PLATEAU Vijayawada
Dharwad Bay of Bengal
Mangalore COROMANDEL COAST
Bangalore Madras
Coimbatore
Cochin
Madurai Jaffna
Trivandrum
SRI LANKA
COLOMBO
Galle

CHINA
HIMALAYAS
MYANMAR
Gandi Res.
DESERT
MALABAR COAST

CHINA AND MONGOLIA

ISOLATED FROM THE western world for centuries, the Chinese were the first to develop the compass, paper, gunpowder, porcelain, and silk. Three autonomous regions lie within western China – Inner Mongolia, Xinjiang, and Tibet. The Gobi desert, in vast Mongolia, is the world's most northern desert.

PEOPLE
Han Chinese make up 93 percent of China's population. China has relaxed its 1979 one-child policy for minority groups, such as the Mongolians, Tibetans, and Muslim Uygurs, after some groups faced near extinction.

HISTORY
Tibet was invaded by China in 1950. The Chinese have destroyed Tibet's traditional agricultural society and Buddhist monasteries. In 1959 there were more than 6,000 monasteries – by 1980, only 179 remained.

KAZAKHSTAN

ALTAI MTS.

L. Us

Har Us I.

XINJIANG UIGHUR

Ürümqi

AUTONOMOUS

TIEN MTS.

Tarim

L. Bosten

REGION

Tarim Basin

Lop Nur

KYRGYZSTAN

TAKLA MAKAN
DESERT

ALTUN MTS.

C

TAJIKISTAN

AFGHANISTAN

KUNLUN MTS.

BAY

PAKISTAN

Aksai
Chin
(Controlled by
China, claimed
by India)

TIBETAN

AUTONOMOUS

TANGGULA MTS.

Demchok
(Claimed by both
China and India)

REGION

GANGDISE RANGE

Brahmaputra (Yarlung Zangbo)

Lhasa

HIMALAYAS

E F G H

SOUTHWESTERN CHINA IS SHOWN ON PP.120-121.

MONGOLIA
P 2.3 million
L Khalkh Mongol

RUSSIAN FEDERATION

L. Hövsgöl

Eg-gyn

SANGARA MTS.

Delger Uldz

Hulun Nur

Amur

Argun

GREATER KHINGAN RANGE

ULAN BATOR

MONGOLIA

INNER MONGOLIA

GOBI DESERT

SEA OF JAPAN

BAIDAN JARAN DESERT

Great Wall

Baotou

Hohhot

ORDOS DESERT

EASTERN CHINA

NORTH KOREA

SOUTH KOREA

Qinghai Hu

Xining

Great Wall

YELLOW SEA

QING HAI MTS.

EASTERN CHINA

CHINA
P 1.2 billion
L Mandarin

INDUSTRY
Coal, tungsten, iron ore, oil.
China is the world's largest coal and
tungsten producer. Grains are grown
in Mongolia on irrigated
land or oases.

CLIMATE
In Mongolia, temperatures can
reach 106°F (41°C) and sometimes drop
to −58°F (−50°C). Northwestern China
is affected by the winter monsoon, which
brings cold, dry air from Siberia.

N

0   400   800km
0   200   400miles

E F G H

CHINA AND KOREA

ONE-FIFTH of the world's population lives in China – mostly in the eastern part of the country. Annexed to Japan in 1910, Korea was divided between the U.S.A. and Communist Russia after World War II. North and South Korea were formed in 1948.

NORTHWESTERN CHINA IS SHOWN ON PP. 118–119.

RUSSIAN FEDERATION

LESSER KHINGAN MTS.

Amur

MANCHURIA

Qiqihar

Harbin

Jilin

Changchun

Chŏngjin

NORTH KOREA

PYONGYANG

Sinŭiju

Namp'o

Fushun

Shenyang

Anshan

Dalian

Bo Hai

Tangshan

Tientsin

Shandong Pen.

YELLOW SEA

Qingdao

Zaozhuang

Nanjing

Wuxi

Shanghai

Hefei

Huainan

Zhengzhou

Handan

Luoyang

Xi'an

Chengdu

Han He

CHINA

JAPAN SEA

Inch'ŏn

SEOUL

Taejŏn

Taegu

Pusan

SOUTH KOREA

Cheju

Korea Strait

Zibo

Jinan

Shijiazhuang

Taiyuan

PEKING

Datong

Great Wall

Yellow River (Huang He)

WESTERN CHINA

NINGXIA HUI AUTONOMOUS REGION

Lanzhou

MONGOLIA

Great Wall

Chang Jiang (Yangtze)

Yangtze

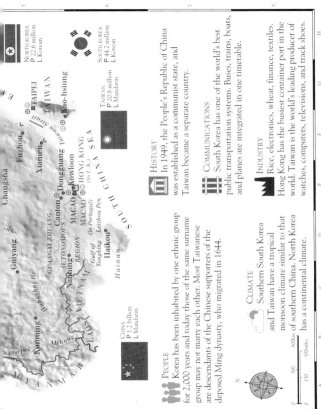

NORTH KOREA
P 22.6 million
L Korean

SOUTH KOREA
P 44.2 million
L Korean

TAIPEI ⊕ TAIWAN
⊕ Kao-hsiung

TAIWAN
P 20.8 million
L Mandarin

Fuzhou

Xiamen ● Dongguang ⊕
Canton ● ⊕ Kowloon
MACAO ⊕ HONG KONG
(to U.K.)

MACAO
(to Portugal)

SOUTH CHINA SEA

GUANGXI ZHUANG
AUTONOMOUS
REGION

Nanning ●

Gulf of
Tonking Leizhou Pen.

Haikou ●

Hainan

Changsha

Guiyang ●

Hechu Hr

VIETNAM

Kunming ●

Mekong

LAOS

Salween

MYANMAR

HISTORY
In 1949, the People's Republic of China was established as a communist state, and Taiwan became a separate country.

COMMUNICATIONS
South Korea has one of the world's best public transportation systems. Buses, trains, boats, and planes are integrated in one timetable.

INDUSTRY
Rice, electronics, wheat, finance, textiles. Hong Kong has the busiest container port in the world. Taiwan is the world's leading producer of watches, computers, televisions, and track shoes.

PEOPLE
Korea has been inhabited by one ethnic group for 2,000 years and today many may not marry those of the same surname group each other. Most Taiwanese are descendants of the Chinese supporters of the deposed Ming dynasty, who migrated in 1644.

CLIMATE
Southern South Korea and Taiwan have a tropical monsoon climate similar to that of southern China. North Korea has a continental climate.

CHINA
P 1.2 billion
L Mandarin

N

0   100   600m
0   150   300miles

JAPAN

CONSISTING OF FOUR main islands and 4,000 smaller ones, Japan is the world's leading industrial nation. Since two-thirds of the land is mountainous, the majority of people live on the coast. Japan has about 1,500 minor earthquakes a year, but severe earthquakes, such as the one in Kobe in 1995, occur every few years. Underwater earthquakes sometimes cause huge surge waves, or *tsunami*, along Japan's Pacific coast.

INDUSTRY

Fishing, ship building, motor vehicles, computers, televisions, high-tech electronics. Motor vehicles are Japan's biggest export, and its stock exchange ranks second in the world. Japan excels at producing

HISTORY

Japan was once ruled by warlords called shoguns, who discouraged contact with the outside world. In 1639, Japan cut ties with other nations and ordered all Europeans to leave, except the Dutch who were allowed one trading ship per year.

La Pérouse Strait

SEA OF OKHOTSK

Kurile Islands

Yekaterina Strait

Iturup Is.

Hokkaidō

TESHIO MTS.

HIDAKA MTS.

Ishikari

Sapporo

Ishikari Bay

Uchiura Bay

Tsugaru Strait

OU MTS.

Sendai

Nagaoki

SEA OF JAPAN

Toyama Bay

JAPAN
P 124.5 million
L Japanese

NATURAL FEATURES

Situated on an unstable part of the Earth's crust, Japan is prone to earthquakes and volcanic activity. There are more than 150 major volcanoes in Japan (over 60 of which are active). These form part of the "Ring of Fire" that runs along the edge of the Pacific Ocean.

CLIMATE

The Sea of Japan has a moderating influence on Japan's climate. Winters are not as cold as on the Asian mainland, and Japan has a much higher rainfall – most of which falls in summer.

COMMUNICATIONS

The *Shinkansen*, or bullet train, is the second fastest in the world. With an average speed of 122 mph (195 km/h), it is renowned for both its speed and reliability.

PEOPLE

The Japanese, both young and old, are avid readers of comic books, known as *manga* and newspapers. Also popular are lifestyle magazines, which encourage the Japanese to make more use of their limited leisure time.

N

0   75   150

0   150km

0   150miles   300km

MAINLAND SOUTHEAST ASIA

FOR MOST of its history, Thailand has been an independent kingdom. Malaysia includes 11 states on the mainland (Malaya), as well as Sabah and Sarawak in Borneo. Cambodia, Laos, and Vietnam have suffered from years of civil war. Myanmar has become more isolated from the world by its repressive government.

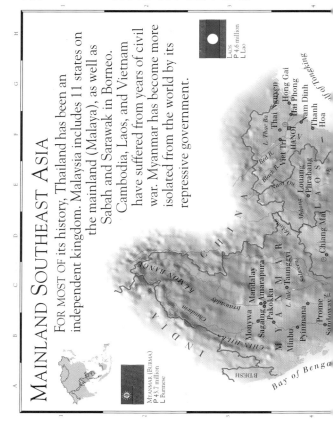

LAOS
P 4.6 million
L Lao

MYANMAR (BURMA)
P 43.7 million
L Burmese

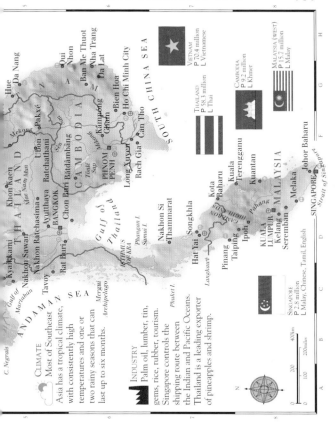

Da Nang · Hue · Qui Nhon · Ban Me Thuot · Nha Trang · Da Lat

V I E T N A M

Pakxé · Bien Hoa · Ho Chi Minh City

Kompong Cham · Can Tho

Mekong

Ubon Ratchathani · Bàtdâmbâng

Khon Kaen · Mae Nam Mun · Sen

Nakhon Sawan · Nakhon Ratchasima · PHNOM PENH · Long Xuyen · Rach Gia

T H A I L A N D · C A M B O D I A

Tonle Sap · Mekong

Ayutthaya · Chon Burí Bàtdâmbâng

BANGKOK

S O U T H   C H I N A   S E A

Ayutthami

G u l f   o f   M a r t a b a n

Tavoy · Bat Burí

ISTHMUS OF KRA

G u l f   o f   T h a i l a n d

Phangan I. · Samui I.

Nakhon Si Thammarat

Phuket I.

A N D A M A N   S E A

Mergui Archipelago

C. Negrais

Kota Baharu · Kuala Terengganu · Kuantan

Songkhla · Hat Yai

Pinang · Baharu

Langkawi · Taiping · Ipoh · Pahang · Kelang

KUALA LUMPUR · Seremban · Melaka

CAMERON HIGHLANDS

M A L A Y S I A

Johor Baharu

SINGAPORE

Strait of Singapore

VIETNAM
P 70.4 million
L Vietnamese

THAILAND
P 58.3 million
L Thai

CAMBODIA
P 9.2 million
L Khmer

MALAYSIA (WEST)
P 15.7 million
L Malay

SINGAPORE
P 2.8 million
L Malay, Chinese, Tamil, English

CLIMATE
Most of Southeast Asia has a tropical climate, with consistently high temperatures and one or two rainy seasons that can last up to six months.

INDUSTRY
Palm oil, lumber, tin, gems, rice, rubber, tourism. Singapore controls the shipping route between the Indian and Pacific Oceans. Thailand is a leading exporter of pineapples and shrimp.

0   100   200   300   400 km
0   100   200 miles

N E S W

MARITIME SOUTHEAST ASIA

SCATTERED BETWEEN the Indian and Pacific Oceans are thousands of tropic mountainous islands. Once called the East Indies, Indonesia was ruled by the Dutch for 350 years. More than half of its 13,677 islands are still uninhabited. The Philippines lie on the "Ring of Fire," and are subject to earthquakes and volcanic activity. Borneo is shared among Indonesia, Malaysia, and Brunei.

BRUNEI
P 280,000
L Malay

SOUTH CHINA SEA

PHI

Balaba
Stra

Kota
Kinabalu

BANDAR SERI
BEGAWAN

BRUNEI

MALAYSIA
(EAST)

SARAWAK

Bor ne

Natuna Is.

Rajang

Simeulue

Medan

L.Toba

Anambas Is.

Strait of
Singapore

Kuching

Kapuas

MULLER MTS.

Samarin

Nias

Sumatra

Lingga

Pontianak

Padang

Batanghari

Singkep

Balikpapa

Siberut

BARISAN MTS.

Bangka

Jambi

Palembang

Belitung

Banjarmasin

JAVA SEA

Tanjungkarang

IN

JAKARTA

Semarang

L

Cirebon

Bogor

Surabaya

Bandung

Kediri

Jember

Yogyakarta

Malang

N

Java

Denpasar

INDIAN   OCEAN

Lombo

MALAYSIA (EAST)
SABAH AND SARAWAK
P 3.4 million
L Malay

0   300   600km
0   150   300miles

INDUSTRY

Palm oil, lumber, rice, oil, natural gas, copper, chrome, tourism. Malaysia is the largest producer of palm oil and computer disk-drives. Indonesia is a major exporter of natural gas.

ENVIRONMENT

Logging, especially in Borneo and the Philippines, is a problem in the region. Forest communities, like the Malaysian Penan, are being destroyed. Some tree species are near extinction.

CLIMATE

Countries situated around the equator are hot and humid all year. Variations in climate are related to latitude.

PHILIPPINES
P 65.6 million
L Filipino, English

INDONESIA
P 187.8 million
L Bahasa Indonesia

on Strait
Luzon
Baguio
Dagupan
es •Cabanatuan
MANILA
Lucena
ngas   Naga
Mindoro •Legaspi
doro
rait
Panay Cadiz
Iloilo
an
Bacolod •Cebu
INES Negros
•Butuan
•Cagayan de Oro
•Iligan Mindanao
Zamboanga •Davao
Jolo General Santos
Sulu Archipelago
Talaud Is.

PHILIPPINE SEA

PACIFIC OCEAN

CELEBES SEA
assar Strait
Manado• Halmahera
Gulf of Tomini Sula Is. Molucca Sea
•Palu
Celebes Supiori
Biak Jayapura
Mamberamo
Seram IRIAN JAYA
Kendari Buru •Ambon MAOKE MTS.
Kai Is. ARAFURA SEA
•Ujung Pandang BANDA SEA Aru Is. Digul
N Dolak
FLORES SEA
mbawa Tanimbar Is.
Flores PAPUA NEW GUINEA
ser Sunda Islands Timor TIMOR SEA
nba Roti Kupang

MOLUCCA SEA
SERÁM SEA
Moluccas

Samar
Calbayog •Tacloban

PACIFIC OCEAN

THE LARGEST AND deepest
ocean, the Pacific covers a
greater area of the Earth's surface
than all the land areas together.
Its deepest point – 36,197ft
(11,033 m) – is deep enough
to cover Mount Everest.
Melanesia, Micronesia,
and Polynesia are the
main inner Pacific
island groups.

MICRONESIA
P 104,000
L English

NAURU
P 9,400
L Nauruan, English

NATURAL FEATURES
Some Pacific islands are
coral atolls – ring-shaped islands
or chains of islands surrounding
a lagoon. They are formed when
coral builds up on a sunken bank or
on a volcano crater in the open sea.

SOLOMON
ISLANDS
P 349,500
L English

ENVIRONMENT
Nuclear testing by the
U.S.A. and France has
dangerously polluted areas in
the South Pacific. Countries
such as Japan, Australia, and
New Zealand want the region
made into a nuclear-free zone.

VANUATU
P 163,000
L Bislama,
English, French

FIJI
P 758,300
L English

N

| 0 | 1500 | 3000km |
| 0 | 750 | 1500miles |

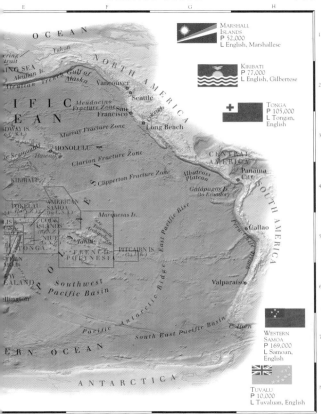

MARSHALL ISLANDS
P 52,000
L English, Marshallese

KIRIBATI
P 77,000
L English, Gilbertese

TONGA
P 105,000
L Tongan, English

WESTERN SAMOA
P 169,000
L Samoan, English

TUVALU
P 10,000
L Tuvaluan, English

OCEAN

Yukon

Bering Strait

KING SEA

Aleutian Trench

Gulf of Alaska

Vancouver

NORTH AMERICA

Seattle

Mendocino Fracture Zone

San Francisco

Colorado

CIFIC

EAN

Long Beach

Murray Fracture Zone

MIDWAY IS. (U.S.A.)

Clarion Fracture Zone

HONOLULU

ie Seamounts

Hawaii

CENTRAL AMERICA

Clipperton Fracture Zone

KIRIBATI

Albatross Plateau

Panama City

Galápagos Is. (to Ecuador)

SOUTH AMERICA

TOKELAU

AMERICAN SAMOA (to U.S.A.)

Marquesas Is.

ISA

COOK ISLANDS (N.Z.)

Callao

East Pacific Rise

Tuamotu Archipelago

Tahiti

NIUE (N.Z.)

Peru-Chile Trench

STERN MOA

TONGA

FRENCH POLYNESIA

PITCAIRN IS. (U.K.)

NEW ZEALAND

Southwest Pacific Basin

Valparaiso

Antarctic Ridge

llington

Pacific

South East Pacific Basin

C. Horn

ERN OCEAN

ANTARCTICA

AUSTRALASIA

NAURU

PAPUA NEW
GUINEA

SOLOMON
ISLANDS

Coral Sea Islands
(to Australia)

VANUATU

New Caledonia
(to France)

AUSTRALIA

TASMAN SEA

SOUTHERN OCEAN

NEW ZEALAND

Auckland Islands
(to N.Z.)

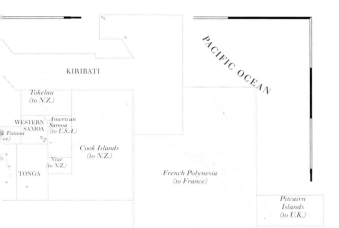

KIRIBATI

Tokelau
(to N.Z.)

WESTERN
SAMOA   *American
Samoa
(to U.S.A.)*
*& Futuna
ce)*

Cook Islands
(to N.Z.)

*Niue
(to N.Z.)*

TONGA

French Polynesia
(to France)

PACIFIC OCEAN

Pitcairn
Islands
(to U.K.)

*Chatham Island
(to N.Z.)*

Australasia

Millions of years ago, the continent of
Australia and the islands of New Guinea
and New Zealand split away from the
other southern continents. These island
countries have many unique plants and
animals, such as Australia's marsupials,
or pouched mammals. The thousands of
islands scattered in the Pacific are either
volcanic islands or coral atolls.

AUSTRALIA AND PAPUA NEW GUINEA

THE SMALLEST, flattest, and driest continent, Australia has a landscape that varies from tropical rainforest to arid desert. Lying to the north, Papua New Guinea (PNG) is so mountainous that its tribes are isolated from each other and from the outside world.

AUSTRALIA
P 17.6 million
L English

TIMOR SEA

Joseph Bonaparte Gulf

DARW
DARN
L.

INDIAN OCEAN

KIMBERLEY PLATEAU

KING LEOPOLD RANGES

Fitzroy

Fi

N O

GREAT SANDY DESERT

TE

North West C.

HAMERSLEY RANGE

L. *Mackay*

A U S T

Alice Spring

L. Disappointment

W E S T E R N

MACDON RANG

GIBSON DESERT

Dirk Hartog I.

A U S T R A L I A

L. *Macleod*

L. Carnegie

GREAT VICTORIA DESERT

L. Barlee

A

L. Moore

NULLARBOR PLAIN

PERTH ⊙

Great Australian

C. Naturaliste

C. Leeuwin

C. Pasley

CLIMATE
Most people live in temperate zones that occur within 250 miles (400 km) of the coast in the east and southeast, and around Perth in the west. The interior, west, and south are arid; the north is tropical. PNG is tropical, yet snow falls on its highest mountains.

INDUSTRY
Coal, gold, uranium, cattle, tourism, wool, wine- and beer-making
Australia is a leading exporter of coal, iron ore, gold, bauxite, and copper, an has the largest known diamond depos
PNG has the largest copper mine in th world and one of the largest gold mine

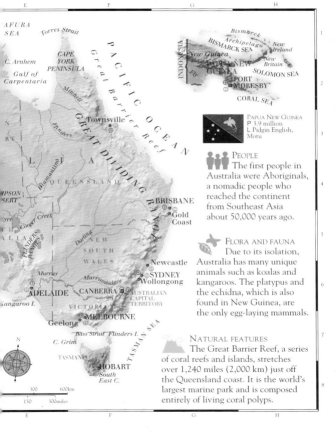

PAPUA NEW GUINEA
P 3.9 million
L Pidgin English,
Motu

PEOPLE

The first people in Australia were Aboriginals, a nomadic people who reached the continent from Southeast Asia about 50,000 years ago.

FLORA AND FAUNA

Due to its isolation, Australia has many unique animals such as koalas and kangaroos. The platypus and the echidna, which is also found in New Guinea, are the only egg-laying mammals.

NATURAL FEATURES

The Great Barrier Reef, a series of coral reefs and islands, stretches over 1,240 miles (2,000 km) just off the Queensland coast. It is the world's largest marine park and is composed entirely of living coral polyps.

NEW ZEALAND

ONE OF THE LAST places on Earth to be inhabited by people, New Zealand lies about halfway between the equator and the South Pole. It is made up of the main North and South Islands, separated by the Cook Strait, and numerous smaller islands. The first settlers were Maoris, who came from the Polynesian islands about 1,200 years ago.

NATURAL FEATURES
New Zealand lies on the "Ring of Fire," a band of volcanic activity that almost encircles the Pacific Ocean. New Zealand has about 400 earthquakes each year, although only about 100 are strong enough to be felt.

PEOPLE
In recent years, Maoris have protested the lack of observance of the Treaty of Waitangi, which protected their rights. About 10 percent of the total population are Maori.

FLORA AND FAUNA
Many of New Zealand's animals have been introduced – two species of bat are the only native land mammals. New Zealand has no snakes.

Great Exhibition Bay

Kaipara Harbour

Auckland

Great Barrier I.

Hamilton

North Island

Bay of Plenty

L. Taupo

Hawke B.

TASMAN SEA

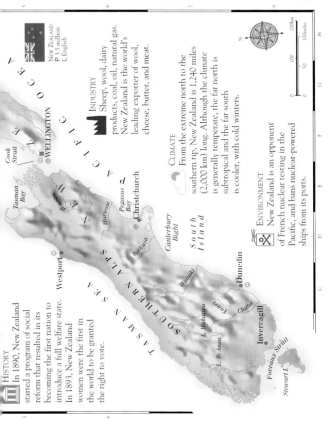

NEW ZEALAND
P 3.5 million
L English

INDUSTRY
Sheep, wool, dairy products, coal, oil, natural gas. New Zealand is the world's leading exporter of wool, cheese, butter, and meat.

CLIMATE
From the extreme north to the southern tip, New Zealand is 1,240 miles (2,000 km) long. Although the climate is generally temperate, the far north is subtropical and the far south is cooler, with cold winters.

ENVIRONMENT
New Zealand is an opponent of French nuclear testing in the Pacific, and bans nuclear-powered ships from its ports.

HISTORY
In 1890, New Zealand started a program of social reform that resulted in its becoming the first nation to introduce a full welfare state. In 1893, New Zealand women were the first in the world to be granted the right to vote.

N

200 miles
100 miles

PACIFIC OCEAN

Cook
Strait

⊕ WELLINGTON

N   O   R   T   H   I   S   L   A   N   D

Tasman Bay

Waiau

TASMAN SEA

Westport

SOUTHERN ALPS

South Island

Rakaia

Hurunui

Pegasus Bay

Christchurch

Canterbury Bight

Waitaki

Dunedin

Clutha

L. Wakatipu

L. Te Anau

Taieri

Invercargill

Foveaux Strait

Stewart I.

Index

Grid references in the Index help find places on the map. If you look up Nairobi in the Index, you will see 96 F4. The first number, 96, is the page number on which the map of Nairobi appears. Next, find the letters and numbers that border the page and trace a line across from the letter and down from the number. This will direct you to the exact grid square in which the city of Nairobi is located.

Miskolc Hungary 71 F6
Mississippi (R.) USA
28 D5/30 D3
Mississippi (State) USA
28 D4
Missouri (R.) USA 33 E2
Missouri (State) USA 33 H5
Mitumba Mts. Zaire 95 G7
Mobile USA 28 D5
Mogadishu Somalia 91 G7
Mojave Desert USA 37 E7
Moldova (Country) 84
Molucca Sea Indonesia
127 F5
Moluccas (Is.) Indonesia
127 F6
Mombasa Kenya 96 G4/
101 C5
Monaco (Country) 63 G7
Mongolia (Country)
118 – 119
Monrovia Liberia 92 C7
Mons Belgium 65 C6
Montana (State) USA
32 D2
Monte Carlo Monaco
63 G7
Montenegro (Republic)
Yugoslavia 75
Monterrey Mexico 39 F4
Montevideo Uruguay
49 E5
Montgomery USA 29 E4
Montpelier USA 27 F4
Montpellier France 63 F7
Montréal Canada 25 E7
Montserrat UK 43 H6
Monywa Myanmar 124 B3
Morava (R.) Czech
Republic/Slovakia 71 D6
Moravia Czech Republic
71 D5
Morocco (Country) 88
Moroni Comoros 101 C5

Moscow Rus. Fed. 83 C5/
112 C4
Mosel (R.) Germany 67 C6
Moselle (R.) France 63 G3
Mostar Bosnia &
Herzegovina 75 D5
Mosul Iraq 109 E2
Moulmein Myanmar
125 C5
Moundou Chad 94 D4
Mozambique (Country)
98 – 99
Muang Phitsanulok
Thailand 125 D5
Mufulira Zambia 97 C6
Mull (I.) UK 58 D3
Multan Pakistan 117 E2
Munich Germany 67 F7
Münster Germany 66 C4
Murcia Spain 61 F6
Murmansk Rus. Fed.
52 G3/82 D3/112 D3
Murray (R.) Australia
133 E6
Murrumbidgee (R.)
Australia 133 F6
Muscat Oman 109 G6
Mwanza Tanzania 96 E4
Mweru, Lake Zambia/
Zaire 97 C5
Myanmar (Country)124
Mykolayiv Ukraine 84 D4

N
N'djamena Chad 94 D4
Naberezhnyye Chelny
Rus. Fed. 83 E6/112 C5
Nacala Mozambique
98 H4
Naga Philippines 127 E2
Nagoya Japan 123 D5
Nagpur India 117 E4
Nain Canada 25 F3
Nairobi Kenya 96 F4

Nakhodka Rus. Fed.
113 E4
Nakhon Ratchasima
Thailand 125 E5
Nakhon Sawan Thailand
125 E5
Nakhon Si Thammarat
Thailand 125 D7
Nam Dinh Vietnam 124 F
Namangan Uzbekistan
111 F3
Namibe Angola 98 A4
Namibia (Country) 99
Nampo'o North Korea
120 G3
Nampula Mozambique
98 H4
Namur Belgium 65 D6
Nanchang China 121 E5
Nancy France 63 F2
Nanjing China 120 F4
Nanning China 121 D6
Nantes France 62 D4
Napier NZ 134 G4
Naples Italy 73 F6
Narsarsuaq Greenland
51 E8
Nashville USA 29 E4
Nasik India 117 E5
Nassau Bahamas 43 E2
Natal Brazil 46 H4
Nauru (Country) 128 D4
Navarin, Cape Rus. Fed.
113 H2
Navoi Uzbekistan 111 E3
Naxos (I.) Greece 79 F6
Ndola Zambia 97 C6
Nebit Dag Turkmenistan
110 C3
Nebraska (State) USA
33 F4
Negro (R.) Brazil 46 C4
Negros (I.) Philippines
127 E3

R

Rabat Morocco 88 D2
Rach Gia Vietnam 125 F6
Rajkot India 116 D4
Rajshahi Bangladesh 117 G4
Raleigh USA 29 G3
Ranchi India 117 F4
Rangoon Myanmar 100 F4/125 C5
Rasht Iran 109 F2
Rat Buri Thailand 125 D5
Rawalpindi Pakistan 117 E1
Reşiţa Romania 76 B4
Recife Brazil 47 H5
Red (R.) China/Vietnam 124 E3
Red Sea 90 E4/100 C3/ 108 D3
Redding USA 37 B5
Regina Canada 23 F8
Reno USA 34 C2
Resistencia Argentina 48 E4
Reykjavik Iceland 52 E3
Rheims France 65 F2
Rhine (R.) W. Europe 64 F4/66 C7/68 C4
Rhode I. (State) USA 27 G5
Rhodes (I.) Greece 79 H7
Rhône (R.) W. Europe 63 F6/68 B6
Richmond USA 29 G2
Riga Latvia 80 D4
Riga, Gulf of Estonia/ Latvia 80 D4
Rîmnicu Vîlcea Romania 76 D4
Río Cuarto Argentina 49 C5
Rio de Janeiro Brazil 47 G6/52 D6

Río Grande (R.) Mexico 39 F3
Rio Grande USA 35 F6
Riverside USA 37 D8
Rivne Ukraine 84 C3
Riyadh Saudi Arabia 109 E5
Roanoke USA 29 G2
Rochester USA 27 E4
Rockford USA 31 E5
Rocky Mts. N. America 22 D6/35 E4
Romania (Country) 76
Rome Italy 73 D5
Rosario Argentina 49 D5
Rostock (Germany) 66 E3
Rostov-na-Donu Rus. Fed. 83 B6/112 B5
Rotterdam Netherlands 52 F4/64 D4
Rouen France 65 E2
Rovuma (R.) C. Africa 98 H4
Rub' al Khali Saudi Arabia 109 E7
Ruse Bulgaria 77 E5
Russian Federation (Country) 81 B5/ 82 – 83/ 112 – 113
Rwanda (Country) 96 D4
Ryazan' Rus. Fed. 83 C5/ 112 C4

S

Saarbrücken Germany 67 C6
Sabah Malaysia 126 D5
Sabhā Libya 89 G4
Sacramento USA 37 B6
Sagaing Myanmar 124 C3
Sahara (Desert) N. Africa 88 – 89/92 – 93
Sahel West Africa 93 E5

Sakhalin (I.) Rus. Fed. 112 H5
Salem USA 36 B4
Salt Lake City USA 34 D2
Salta Paraguay 48 C3
Salton Sea USA 37 E8
Salvador Brazil 47 H5
Salween (R.) Myanmar/ China 119 E7/121 B5/ 124 C4
Salzburg Austria 69 F3
Samar (I.) Philippines 127 F3
Samara Rus. Fed. 83 D6/112 C5
Samarinda Indonesia 126 D6
Samarkand Uzbekistan 111 E4
Sambre (R.) Belgium/ France 65 D6
Samos (I.) Greece 79 G5
Samsun Turkey 105 F3
San'a Yemen 109 E8
San Antonio USA 35 G7
San Bernardo Chile 49 B5
San Diego USA 37 D8
San Francisco USA 37 B6
San José Costa Rica 42 C7
San Jose USA 37 B7
San Juan Puerto Rico 45 G5
San Luis Potosí Mexico 39 F5
San Marino (Country) 72 D4
San Miguel de Tucumán Argentina 48 C4
San Salvador de Jujuy Paraguay 48 C3
San Salvador El Salvador 42 B5
Sanandaj Iran 109 F2

Acknowledgments

Dorling Kindersley would like to thank:
Hilary Bird, Helen Chamberlain, Tricia Grogan, and Michael Williams for the index; Kate Eager and Tony Chung for design assistance; Sasha Heseltine for editorial assistance; Caroline Brooke and Paul Donnellon for editorial research; James Mills-Hicks and Yak El-Droubie for cartographic assistance.

Picture credits: t=top b=bottom c=center l=left r=right
The publisher would like to thank the following for their kind permission to reproduce the photographs:

NASA, 13 tr; Science Photo Library/David Parker 15 br.

Every effort has been made to trace the copyright holders and we apologize in advance for any unintentional omissions. We would be pleased to insert the appropriate acknowledgment in any subsequent edition of this publication.